I0366775

THE INDIAN WHO MOVED BACK

A memoir of his World in the US and India of Semiconductors, Computers, Networks, AI, ERP, Multimedia, Charity, Zen, Advaita, and Nirvana!

THE INDIAN WHO MOVED BACK

A memoir of his World in the US and India of Semiconductors, Computers, Networks, AI, ERP, Multimedia, Charity, Zen, Advaita, and Nirvana!

Dr. Varish Panigrahi

BLACK EAGLE BOOKS
Dublin, USA | Bhubaneswar, India

 Black Eagle Books
USA address:
7464 Wisdom Lane
Dublin, OH 43016

India address:
E/312, Trident Galaxy, Kalinga Nagar,
Bhubaneswar-751003, Odisha, India

E-mail: info@blackeaglebooks.org
Website: www.blackeaglebooks.org

First International Edition Published by
Black Eagle Books, 2025

THE INDIAN WHO MOVED BACK
by **Dr. Varish Panigrahi**

Copyright © Dr. Varish Panigrahi

All rights reserved. No part of this publication may be reproduced, stored in a retrieval system, or transmitted, in any form or by any means, electronic, mechanical, photocopying, recording or otherwise without the prior permission of the publisher.

Cover & Interior Design: Ezy's Publication

ISBN- 978-1-64560-763-2 (Paperback)

Printed in the United States of America

Dedication

Life is a sacred and unique journey where we reinvent ourselves every moment and look forward to receiving all the things life brings, regardless of time and place. This book is dedicated to the memory of all the families, friends, and colleagues who touched my life during my journey in India and the United States of America.

Contents

PREFACE		**11**
Part I: Student Days (1945-1973)		**17**
1.	**Village world**	19
	Bodoboranga	
	Surangi	
	Village School Days	
	Summer Visits	
2.	**World of the Princely State**	34
	Balangir	
	LP School	
	PR High School	
	Rajendra College	
3.	**NIT and IIT World**	51
	NIT Rourkela	
	IIT Kharagpur	
	IIT Campus Life	
4.	**University of Illinois**	62
	Travel to America	
	Life on the American Campus	
	Master's Program	
	Doctoral Program	
5.	**On the Road to Marriage**	69
	Early Marriage Proposal	
	Long Engagement	
	Marriage	
Part II: Work Years in America (1973 to 1997)		**83**
6.	**Life in America**	85
	Living in Piscataway, NJ	
	Living in East Windsor, NJ	
	Living in Branchburg, NJ	
	Living in Westborough, MA	

7. **World of Semiconductors**   98
   Burroughs Corporation (1973 – 1976)
   RCA Solid State Division (1979 – 19981)
   DEC LSI Division (1981 – 1987)
8. **World of Computers**   108
   Burroughs Corporation (1973 – 1976)
   DEC Disk Subsystems (1987 – 1990)
   DEC High Performance Systems (1990 – 1991)
   Data General Corporation (1996)
9. **World of Data Networks**   114
   Bell Laboratories Data Networks (1976 – 1979)
   DEC Personal Computer Networks (1991 – 1992)
   Process Software Corporation (1993 – 1996)
10. **World of Artificial Intelligence**   121
11. **Move from America to India**   124
    Choosing an Indian City
    Building a Residence in India
    Timing the Move

Part III: Work Years in India (1997-2010)   135
12. **PanNet Computer**   137
    Company Formation and First Year
    Multimedia Development
    Computer and Networking Services
    Training Products and Services
    Pattern Recognition and AI Products
    ERP Products and Services
    Restructuring PanNet Computer
13. **World of Technical Education**   151
    Barapada Institute of Engineering Technology
    Biju Patnaik National Steel Institute
14. **A Miraculous Escape**   159

15. Life During the Work Years in India   164
    Living at IRC Village, Bhubaneswar
    Supporting Arun's Education in America
    Living at VIP Colony, Bhubaneswar
    Engagement and Marriage of Arun

Part IV: Retirement Years in India (2010 -2025)   177
16. World of Charity and Social Work   179
    Purusottam Trust
    SriHari Trust
    Ekamrakshetra Rotary
    Sunday Morning School
    School for Slum Children
17. Zen, Advaita, and Writing   187
    Kalinga ZEN Advaita Mahasangha
    Writings on Zen
    Research on Dharmic Religions
    Advaita Dhyana Kalaasangha
    Writings on the Buddha
18. World of Business Mentorship   196
    Blackstar Graphite
    Ashiana Lagoon Trust
    Amruut Foods
19. Revisiting My World   204
    My Other Places Revisited
    Last Trip to America and Some Thoughts
    My Technical World Revisited
20. The Road to Nirvana!   237
    My Beautiful Small City
    Trips in India and Abroad
    Retirement Life
    My Zen Rituals
    Further To Walk

Photographs   261

PREFACE

As I complete eighty years of my life, there has been an urge to look back and put down in pen and paper the long road traversed. I have lived and worked in many different surroundings, technical and non-technical areas. Yet, I have not lost touch with all these different worlds that I had the opportunity to experience and live with. I am carrying all these different worlds in my thoughts and dreams as if they are coalesced together into a single tapestry of light and color.

My journey started in a small village in southern Odisha. And then, suddenly, I got transplanted to a district headquarters town of a princely state in western Odisha, where I had all my schooling. The one-year stint at NIT-Rourkela and then the four-year study at IIT-Kharagpur were the culmination of my dream to fulfill my fascination with the emerging field of electronics technology. The path to a doctoral study program at the University of Illinois Urbana-Champaign and subsequent work years in different facets of electronics, computer, and communication technologies for about two dozen years came as a natural progression.

The move back to India, after almost three decades in the United States of America, was a hard decision that was carried out over a period of ten years for the overall long-term happiness and prosperity of the family. The work years in India allowed me to fulfill my dream of serving Odisha and India, both as an entrepreneur and otherwise.

Retirement life in India offered a unique set of opportunities to further traverse new paths and dreams that I had never fathomed earlier. Hopefully, the years ahead will be as rewarding and peaceful!

The urge to write this autobiography crystallized in the year 2023 as the news of the demise of Professor Jitendra Nath Mohanty in Pennsylvania came about. I had only met Prof. Mohanty once around 1975, when he was working at the New School in New York City. I learned that he was the most brilliant philosopher produced by Odisha and Bengal. The autobiography, 'Between Two Worlds: East and West', I learned about and tried to get hold of a copy without much success for quite a while. But I started writing my story immediately, realizing that I had traversed through many different worlds. It has been more than a year and a half since then, and I continued writing my story intermittently as I was writing and reviewing the book, 'Zen Buddhism and Advaita Vedanta: A Comparative Study'. I had more concentrated time to complete the writing of this autobiography after the publication of that book in the summer of 2024. It was just the inspiration that I got from learning about Professor Mohanty's book and his two worlds, and in no way, my story and the life depicted here have much in common with his life and work.

I have divided this book into four parts. The first part covers my story until I completed my Ph.D. at the University of Illinois. The second part covers the work years in the United States of America. Instead of writing chronologically the different organizations and firms that I worked with and the associated activities, I have lumped them into the four main technical areas: Semiconductors, Computers, Data Networks, and Artificial Intelligence. The third part covers my entrepreneurial and other work experiences in India. The fourth part includes my activities during the retirement years.

This autobiography is written so that there is some written record of the history of the families and friends and the places associated with and possibly to inspire the coming generations. I have not seen any history of the villages around where I was born, and I have tried to record what I have heard and seen. I do not have the opportunity now to talk to my older brothers and sister who saw more and knew more, since they are all gone from this world.

Millions of Indians have emigrated to different countries of the world in the twentieth and twenty-first centuries. Only a few of them have come back after three decades of life overseas. Though my story is a unique case, it may help some better plan their lives moving from India or back to India. My overall experience of the three decades and thereafter in the United States of America was a good one, and in no way, the family's moving back imply the denigration of American social and work cultures. But just that, I had a higher calling from the bottom of my heart to do my part for the betterment of the motherland and be closer to the family and friends in India.

There are, of course, special characteristics of Indian society that make it an attraction. Although Indian society at present is one of the most dynamic in the world in terms of the extent of changes happening, residential structures and practices are oriented toward permanence. Once people move to a new locality and a new residence, they tend to stay there for a lifetime. This enables people to have a strong sense of belonging to a particular place and locality and gives an air of security. In contrast, American society is constantly on the move. People change their residences every seven years on average. This does not sustain long-term relationships. Moving to India, I have stayed in the same locality in Bhubaneswar for three decades. Though Bhubaneswar is a second-tier metropolis, it also feels like a small town and a village around our particular areas. I love this aspect of Indian society in contrast to American society.

The extent of diversity in India in terms of language, religion, culture, food, dress, and terrain is unparalleled in the world. This range of diversity makes life in India very challenging and interesting.

Operating a business enterprise, on the other hand, is very difficult in India. No doubt, things are much better now compared to the situation three decades ago. The diversity of India makes it a huge marketing challenge for business enterprises to sell their wares and services. Each state and the regions within have to be separately considered for any marketing plan. This is a complete contrast to the United States of America, where the whole country is available as a single market.

The infrastructure situation in India was very poor three decades ago and has improved greatly over the last three decades. I had to make provision for intermittent water and electricity. Internet cost and performance were unsatisfactory. So was the situation for landline and mobile phones. The internet and mobile phone connections at present are available with the latest technology. I am happy to note that in our present house, where I have lived for the last two decades, I have been able to build all the conveniences and more compared to my houses in the United States of America. The three levels of terraces and balconies that are built into the house provide a big opportunity for me to go up and down every hour to take breaks from my writing jaunts. The plot sizes are very small in India compared to my one-acre plot house in New

Jersey. But, even with a plot size of 5400 square feet only, I have been able to squeeze in a small pool, lawn in the front, back, and one side, and enough fruit trees, such as custard apples, Lichis, guavas, berries, Sapota, pomegranates, lemon, etc., on the periphery of the house. Of course, flowers and vegetables are being raised at all levels of the house, as much as possible. So, one can make provisions for a much better house or apartment in India compared to those in the United States of America, except for the plot and lawn sizes. It is not surprising that my grandkids, on their extensive visits to India, like it so much here!

The fact that the Government of India, during the year 2024, has identified semiconductors, electronics, and networking products as key strategic sectors for investment has made a huge difference in the introduction of these technologies in India. The dreams of my youth for India are being fulfilled. So, this is an exciting time to be an old electronics and computer professional in India now!

Lastly, I want to thank all my friends who encouraged me to write this memoir, and especially, Shashibhusan Rath. I thank my publishers for their timely and excellent support.

Dr. Varish Panigrahi
drvpanigrahi@aol.com, Mob 91-9437506237
VIP Colony, Plot 7, Nayapally, Bhubaneswar -751015
President, Kalinga ZEN Foundation Trust
President, Advaita Dhyana Kalaasangha

Part I
The Student Days
(1945 to 1973)

01. Village World
02. World of the Princely State
03. NIT and IIT World
04. University of Illinois
05. On the Road to Marriage

1. Village World

Bodoboranga

In the early hours of a hot summer night on 6th May 1945, I was born in the village of Bodoboranga in the Ganjam district of Odisha. The village is situated on the side of the river Bahuda (with a soft 'd') as the river takes a southerly turn near the border with the state of Andhra Pradesh. Bahuda is the smallest of the eleven rivers that flow through Odisha and enter the Bay of Bengal, and is about ninety km long. Two hundred families lived in the village. It was part of the Chikiti Zamindari. The Raja of Chikiti had his palace and fort in Chikiti gada, about eight km away. Patrapur was the nearest large village with the government offices and the post office, and was one km away through the cultivated fields. Patrapur was on the road connecting to Icchapuram, a railway station on the South Eastern Railway, and hence was a terminal point of the journey to Bodoboranga. One had to brave through the fields to reach the village from Patrapur in the rainy and harvest season, when there was not even a way for the bullock carts to go through the fields. Another way to start the journey from the village to catch the train was to go to Icchapuram after crossing the river Bahuda through muddy roads along a few villages in Odisha and Andhra Pradesh. It was about six to seven km this way, and a bullock cart could be prepared to transport family members to the railway station in fair weather, provided there was not much water in the river.

As one entered Bodoboranga from the western end, two rows of houses stretched on the northern and southern sides, separated by more than a hundred feet of open space in between. This was the big front side or 'Danda', which was used by the villagers for all the social and economic activities. My father, Hari Panigrahi, was a land-owning Brahmin who had about twenty acres of land spread out at various places around the village. Like most of the villagers, he owned land on the south side of the river Bahuda. During the rainy season, the river would have anywhere from three to five feet of water flowing through the main stream of the river, and it would be very difficult to go to the other side of the river. There were no bridges in the river nearby, and one had to go all the way about ten kilometers to Icchapuram to cross the river.

I was the youngest child in the family. My two elder brothers were engaged in business in a town in western Odisha, and my third brother was in the village helping out my father in farming. My only sister was married off in a village, a couple of km away on the other side of the river.

My father had two younger brothers and their families who lived in the village and were engaged in farming too. There were at least three other families in the village who belonged to our clan (Vansa), being related to us in a paternal pyramidal structure. There were a few other families of the clan outside the village in Patrapur, Surangi, and Chhatrapur within the Ganjam district of Odisha. The girls were always married outside the clan, and unfortunately, their relationships kind of got erased after one or two generations, since they were out of the clan relations.

Our village had the Radhakrishna monastery (mutt) on the western end and the Shiva temple on the eastern side.

I understand that the Shiva temple was built by a wealthy family from a neighboring village who had lent money to many of the people in our village. He was not able to collect the repayment from the villagers. So, some people, including my father, suggested that he should donate all that money to build a Shiva temple in the village. So, everyone felt duty-bound to pay back the money that was being used for the construction of the temple. An amount of land was also allotted to the temple for the annual maintenance of the temple. My father was in charge of the management of this temple and made sure that the temple land was cultivated and the deity was given the right amount of paddy crops after the harvest, so that daily puja could be done by the 'Raula', who performed the rituals every morning and evening.

The Radhakrishna mutt had a full-time 'Mahanta', who managed all the properties associated with the mutt and also took care of the daily rituals of the deities Radha and Krishna. The Mahanta was a celibate Brahmin by caste and was usually appointed for life at the demise of a serving Mahanta. Since the mutt had a vast account of properties, there were always aspiring persons for the position. Since one had to be celibate for life to be a Mahanta, many did not want to take that route. One had to be inclined to serve the deity and lead in the religious festivals for the people around the mutt.

There is no known history of the village as to wherefrom the original people of the village came here. From the folk stories, we had heard that the village was originally situated near the Barahi temple, one km away, but moved to the present site many generations back after a cruel epidemic that wiped away a big portion of the populace.

My earliest recollection of the village is one where I was being pulled by other kids on the wooden four-wheeler cart. When the cart became inoperative because the axle broke, I took it to the family carpenter in the village. The old man said that he would only fix, if I could tell him all the conjugate alphabets (Yuktakshara) of the Odia language. I must have been in the kindergarten or 'Shishu' grade in the village school at the time. I knew many of those conjugate letters, but not all of them, and had to go back and recite all of them later on. He then fixed my wooden cart.

Surangi

My other recollection of the early years is when I walked with my mother, Hema Panigrahi, to her ancestral village of Surangi. We had to walk about two km between the fields to go to the village of Kelhua, which was on the road from Icchapuram to Surangi. We missed the bus when we arrived there, and my mother decided to walk on the road to her village, which was about six km away. I remember being carried by my mother for some distance. We had to cross the areas of forest and mountains on one side of the road. I remember being apprehensive about the leopard that I had heard of being in those jungles. We finally reached Surangi, and I could see the small hospital building that was at the edge of the village.

Surangi was also called a 'gada' (fort) since it was the capital of a small zamindari at that name, ruled by a Raja, and the palace was located within the walls of a fortlike structure surrounded by high walls. The fort was at the other end of the village, just adjacent to two mountains, which gave it additional protection on the east and south sides. Because of the high mountains on the east side, Surangi was under its shade until about 8 AM. As one entered Surangi from the northern side road, there was a wide road about two hundred feet wide, and on both sides of the road, there were about eight to ten monasteries (mutt or 'Matha' in Odia). Each of these mutts had a wide concrete building with a temple room for the deity, a spacious courtyard, gardens, store rooms, and rooms for the 'Mahanta' (the chief priest) and some of his staff. At the end of this wide road was the palace fort. The first mutt on the right side, next to the palace fort, was the one where my eldest maternal uncle was the Mahanta. We called him 'Babaji Mamu' (Monkish Uncle), and we were always eager to meet him after arriving at the ancestral house of my grandfather.

My maternal grandfather, Ramachandra Panigrahi, was in charge of the revenue department of the Raja of Surangi. He had at one time three sons, and hence he made his eldest son the Mahanta of the mutt next to the palace. It so happened that his other two young sons would die in an epidemic, and he would wish God to give him another son. My mother was the youngest of the three daughters of my grandfather. The oldest daughter was married to someone in the same village, but became a child widow around the age of ten. In those times, there was no remarriage of the Brahmin girls. After some time, my grandfather arranged to send his eldest daughter as part of the entourage that was sent as a gift when the princess of the kingdom of 'Manjusha' (an area in Andhra Pradesh in Srikakulam district, but adjacent to Ganjam district and the king being of Odia ancestry) was married off in distant Balangir Patna State in western Odisha. The princess was married to the younger brother of King Prithvi Raj Singh. Thus, my mother's eldest sister moved to Balangir as part of the family of Lal Saheb, the brother of Prithvi Raj Singh. She was in charge of the kitchen stock room and was known as 'Sarani-Nani'. Her presence in Balangir would open a whole new avenue for our family, especially for my elder brothers and me, as will be told in the next chapter.

My maternal grandfather finally had another son, and he was the youngest child of the family and would inherit the family wealth and position. My mother's other sister, who was married off and had a child, was abandoned by her husband, who left home to become a holy man. Her young daughter died, and she came back to live with my grandparents. Thus, only one of the daughters and one of the sons grew up to have families of their own. My two elder brothers and sister grew up in Surangi with the grandparents, since they were the only grandchildren at the time. There was an upper primary school in Surangi, and hence all of them studied up to the fifth standard there in Surangi. My eldest brother, Koramoni (Koranna), studied at Chikiti Middle School for a few years and then went to Balangir to study in high school. He followed my younger uncle, who had earlier gone to Balangir to complete his high school education. My sister, Subasini (Subasa Abba), also studied in Surangi and grew up there. My second brother, Padma Charan (Padmanna), did not study after his education at Surangi, and after a brief stint at our village helping our father, would also go to Balangir to join my eldest brother in business.

Village School Years

Myself and my third brother, Rupa Chandra (Rupanna), grew up in Bodoboranga and went to study at the school there. The school was a thatched hut in the middle of the village. There was one large room where all the classes were held. When my third brother finished third grade, he was sent to the school in Patrapur, which was about one kilometer away, going through the rice fields. There was no road connecting the village with Patrapur, and it was difficult to go through the fields during the season when paddy was being harvested in the fields. My brother was not interested in studies and stopped going to school in Patrapur in the middle of the fourth grade. He was eight years older and was the big brother who helped my father manage the fields and arrange the different activities. Thus, I almost grew up alone at home and was very close to my mother as the youngest child. I remember every morning collecting flowers for my mother from around the Thakurani temple, which was at the end of the village.

The village school was a very hospitable environment since two of my second cousins were the teachers in the school, the elder one being the headmaster. We went to the school every morning at around 7.00 AM and studied up to 10 AM. The morning period was spent doing only arithmetic. We only brought a slate and a hard chalk to write on it. We wrote the multiplication tables from 1 to 25 times ten every morning, while sometimes chanting as we wrote. Once this exercise was completed in the morning, there would be questions asked by the teacher to test whether we knew the multiplication table. Often, the teacher would provide a problem to be solved by the class. I do not remember having a book on mathematics while I was in the village school until the end of the second grade.

After coming from the morning school, I remember dropping off my pants and shirt at home and running to the river. We would defecate in the field next to the riverside and then go to the river to clean and bathe. After playing in the water for at least fifteen minutes, I would run home. All the houses in the village were designed such that the width was only ten to twenty feet, but they were long like a bunch of train compartments. Our house had six cemented rooms and two rooms at the back of mud walls that were used for cooking and eating. The back side of the house was to the riverside. The river was the constant companion where we went to relieve ourselves and bathe, during the days and the evenings. Except at the time of the flood in the rainy season, there was mostly a couple of feet of water, and hence it was not risky to bathe and play in the river Bahuda. During the rainy season, there will be floods, and we can see the water all around us. The water will come up to the front road from both ends of the village. Often, wild streams of water would encircle the village by finding an alternate path around the village.

The afternoon school started from around 3.30 PM and continued for two hours until 5.30 PM. We studied a class book that was prescribed at the beginning of the year. Thus, the afternoons were spent on reading, and the teacher made sure that the students were reading aloud. One could hear the sound of the fifty students reading aloud in the afternoon.

There were a few girls in the class. But their number would decrease starting from the second grade, since many of them would be married off after the age of eight and be waiting at home to be sent to their in-laws' house when they started menstruation at the age of eleven to thirteen. There would be a short ceremony at the bride's house, and then she would be sent to the groom's family along with gifts for the household, and there would be a welcome ceremony at the groom's house. Girl students did not come back to the school after marriage. So, I remember some of my girl schoolmates dropping off in second grade since they were married. Poor male students also started dropping off in the second grade since they had to start working in the fields to help the family.

There was one elaborate celebration on the day of Saraswati Puja in the winter months. That was the day many of the new students would formally enter the kindergarten by performing puja by first writing on the slate with chalk. They had to be at least four years and four months old to go through this ceremony. All the students would get some gifts for the teachers. In addition, the headmaster would select one of the students as the one who holds the symbol of Saraswati, 'Shreephala', and the teachers, along with the student, would go around the village to the student's family, and the parents would give gifts for this special honor of the student. I was chosen in the second grade for this honor, and I remember walking to my maternal uncle's house in Surangi along with the teachers to get gifts from my uncle's family. This was a tradition of providing annual gifts to the teachers and persisted even in the government schools, where teachers were paid salaries from the government.

The schools were closed for a couple of weeks toward the end of December every year, and we were told that it was for the celebration of the paddy harvest. The students were supposed to help their families with cutting the paddy crops, and then help process them and store the paddy underground in front of everyone's house. At the end of this celebration, sweets made out of puffed rice were available for sale and distribution from the families, who were engaged in the trade of selling sweets.

We had a pair of male buffalo that were used to pull the wooden cart, which was used for the transportation of manure, paddies, hay, etc. When the family had to travel to a distant village or go to Icchapuram to take the train, the cart would be fitted with a special half-round bamboo frame cover so that four to six adults and children could sit inside comfortably. The pair of buffalo was used for the heavy pulling of the cart for the short and long haul. We had three pairs of bullocks, and they were mainly used for tilling the land. The bullocks were sometimes used for light transport with the help of a cart.

I remember participating in these harvest activities. During the paddy cutting season, as the hired hands cut the paddy and pile it up, they also drop off strands of paddy in the field. So, my responsibility was to collect the remnant paddy strands together. I remember bringing a whole big collection of these paddy stands as my labor output and giving it to my mother at the end of the day. I often went with my father and the servants to the fields and knew all of the pieces of land the family owned by name and location.

I especially remember during my second grade in the village, my father took me along with him walking to Patrapur, which was one km away through the fields. In Patrapur, there was an open field where there were booths, and my father spent some time around these booths, and then we walked back to the village. My father did not tell me what was going on in these booths, but much later, I understood that it was perhaps the first general election that was held in the year 1952, after the new constitution was adopted in India. There was not much campaigning in those days in the villages, and only a few people came to vote in the adjoining block offices at the block headquarters. Our village was within the Patrapur election block, and hence we had to walk up to the polling booths there.

As part of entertainment in the evening, I went along with my mother to listen to the recital of Ramayana and Mahabharata in front of the front porch of one of the neighbors. He would recite the text for the ladies and men to hear at around 8 PM, after everyone had their evening meals. I attended these every day in summer evenings with my mother. By the time I was in the second grade, I had heard all these stories from the Ramayana and the Mahabharata. My mother did not know how to read and write, since the girls in her time did not attend school in rural areas. But she knew the whole of Ramayana and Mahabharata just like all the people in the village. Although most of them had not gone to any school and did not know how to read and write, they all could say what was right and wrong from their knowledge of these mythical stories. When she woke up early in the morning, she prepared the food for the cows, bullocks, and buffalo, if there was any to be given. She would also collect the milk by pulling the nipples of cows, if there was a new young calf in the cowshed. The cowshed was in a building amongst the row of houses behind our main house. Other well-off families also had their cowshed in this back row of the village. There were two washerman families in the village, and their houses were also in this row. Behind this row of houses, there was another row of houses right up to the edge of the river, where half a dozen families lived who were at the time considered untouchables and were engaged in various trades. Some of them were also employed as servants of the rich farmers, but were not allowed to come inside the houses of the masters.

During the late spring, in the month of March/April, a three-day festival was observed at a place a kilometer northwest of the village where the river Bahuda had a sharp turn to the right. There was a temple of the goddess Barahi at the site. Traders and villagers from around about fifty villages in the area would gather here to buy different household goods offered by the merchants at the stalls. In the evening, there would be different shows and performances until the early morning. I remember seeing the play, Hiranyakashyapa and Prahlad, being enacted one late evening. Separate teams from each village came here during the day and evening to perform different songs, bhajans, and kirtan performances. The villagers prepared for this festival for months after the harvest. They would practice the plays around the stories of Krishna and Rama in the village and then get the chance to present them at this annual festival. This Barahi 'Buda' (bathing in the river) festival was the joint effort of all the surrounding villages and had been going on for many generations.

    I left the village at the age of eight in the summer of 1953 to start the third grade in the distant Balangir town in western Odisha. My two elder brothers were engaged in business there. My eldest brother had studied up to matriculation at the high school in Balangir and had stayed there to do business, after having a couple of years of government jobs as a clerk and a school teacher. He had prospered in the business there. My maternal uncle's eldest son, Prafulla, studied there since his second grade. So, I was eager to go to Balangir and stay at my eldest brother's house. No doubt, it was a good decision since there was no high school close by to attend classes while staying with the parents in the village.

    I left the village along with my eldest brother when he came to the village in the summer. We went to Icchapuram to take the train from there to Vizianagaram. From there, we had to board another train going towards Raipur. We had to get down at Titlagarh railway station and from there take a bus going to Balangir.

Summer Visits

My living in the village came to an end in the summer of 1953. After that, I would visit the village during the summer season every couple of years. Since it was so distant and took a couple of days of travel to come from Balangir to the village, I never came in between the academic sessions unless there was an occasion for some special family event or celebration. Whenever I came to the village in the summertime, I would go to the southern side of the river where there was always a 'ganda' (deep water) across the bed of the river. Some years it stretched almost 500 meters along the river bed. This was produced during the flood season, depending on the severity of the current in the river during the floods. I would gather on the other side of this deep section, where there was always a mound of sand. Some of the junior students who were enrolled in the schools and colleges in the surrounding area would accompany me there. Most of my classmates and people in my age group were too busy with their farming occupations. Of course, the work schedule during the summer months was more relaxed, and the farmers were busy during this time to prepare the land for the next set of crops starting in the rainy season. During this time, they would distribute in the field the cow manure collected during the year at the cowsheds. Herds of goats and rams would be on rent to stay the nights on particular fields, so that they naturally fertilize the particular piece of land. These herds generally came with their owners from the villages in Andhra Pradesh.

Whenever I came to the village in the summer, I would also go to Surangi to meet my maternal uncles and cousins and spend a couple of days. Two of my uncle's sons were about the same age, and the eldest one had already spent his second and third grades in Balangir. They were all enrolled in a high school, which started near Patrapur. We all would bathe late morning in the pond that was along the side of the palace fort in Surangi. We would also visit first the mutt next to the pond, where my eldest uncle was the Mahanta. He was a lifelong celibate and was very cordial and entertaining. Whenever I went there with my elder brothers in the evening, he would also serve us special drinks mixed with "Bhang" (a herb similar to hashish). The young ones got smaller portions of these drinks. His mutt included a room for the deity and an adjoining complex of rooms for his living. There was also a cowshed and a garden. The mutt owned cultivated land around Surangi, and sharecroppers tilled this land and gave a portion of the harvested crops to the mutt. That was the main source of income that was needed for the upkeep and maintenance of the mutt.

Unfortunately, the mutt turned into a dilapidated state after my elder uncle's death. One of my cousins was anointed to become the Mahanta of the mutt, but he did not pursue that path and became a householder, and had other pursuits after getting his college degree. The cultivated land of the mutt has been appropriated by the sharecroppers, despite the legal cases against them lodged by my younger uncle. This is also the story of many of the other mutts in Surangi and those still dot both sides of the wide road (Badadanda) in the village. A chariot festival is usually held here, as in Puri, and the three deities, Jagannath, Balabhadra, and Subhadra, would come out of the temple inside the palace fort and go up to the other end of the road and then come back to their permanent abode after about ten days on the day of 'Bahuda'. I participated in a few of these chariot festivals in Surangi during the summers.

Surangi was always a more modern village since it was connected by the road to Berhampur through Icchapuram. This part of Odisha was part of the Madras Presidency since the early nineteenth century, and Berhampur was the farthest official outpost of the Madras Presidency and had sizable Telugu and Tamil communities. On the first of April 1936, Odisha province was established in British India by joining the western, eastern, and southern parts respectively from Bombay, Calcutta, and Madras presidencies. This was the first such province established according to language in India, in this case, Odia. The Odia people were the first to rebel against British rule more than two hundred years ago in the year 1817. This uprising is called the 'Paika' rebellion, and it was led by Bakshi Jagabandhu Bidyadhar, the Commander-in-Chief of the Khurdah fort associated with the king of Puri and Khurdah. The British had kept the Odia nation in check by keeping them in three separate parts until 1st April 1936.

After the independence of India, the Surangi administrative services were later merged with India. My uncle had the revenue department of the estate from his father and was eventually absorbed as a Revenue Inspector in the state government service and served across the various locations in the Ganjam district. The Surangi zamindari, ruled by a Raja, finally acceded to Odisha State on 1st June 1953. The Chikiti Zamindari also acceded to Odisha on the same date.

2. World of the Princely State

It was the summer of the year 1953. India had been independent of British rule for about half a dozen years. The new constitution of India was adopted, and India became a republic on January 26th, 1951. The first general election of the country to choose the members of the parliament and the state assemblies was held in the year 1952. There was an air of nationalism and optimism in the new republic. Balangir was the capital of the Balangir Patna Princely State, ruled by a Maharaja, who earlier owed his allegiance to the British throne, but had acceded to the newly created union of India.

Balangir

I left my village of Bodoboranga to go to Balangir in the summer of the year 1953. I reached the town of Balangir after a day-long train journey from Icchapuram to Vizianagaram and from there to Titlagarh, and then through a state transport bus to Balangir. Taking a rickshaw, I reached my brother's house in the Rugudipara area of the town. Balangir was then a small town with a population of about fifteen thousand. It was a relatively new town that had only started in the middle of the sixteenth century CE and expanded in the nineteenth century. The Patna state was established by Ramai Deo of the Chauhan dynasty in the year 1360 CE. Other adjoining kingdoms were the Sambalpur State, Sonepur State, and the zamindaris of Khariar and Jarasingha. The capital of Patna State was originally at Patnagarh, and there are remnants of the palace and the fort there. The Chauhan dynasty had set up a string of eighteen such states in western Odisha. Narasingha Deo had handed over the area north of the river Ong to his brother Balaram Deo. Balaram moved his capital from Patnagarh to a more central location about 40km east of Patnagarh, and this was called Balaramgarh. During the British administration, Balaramgarh became Balangir over the years.

The modern town of Balangir was built after it was sanctioned in 1872 by the British administration. In the middle of the town, there existed the old palace grounds where the descendants of the royal family lived. There was a planned town area where roads were placed in a grid pattern, and the houses were constructed on the plots adjoining the roads. A series of half a dozen interconnected ponds was constructed along the length of the town to provide water to the residents.

An English school was started in 1894 by Maharaja Ramachandra Singh Deo. King Dalganjan Singh Deo succeeded him, and his son Prithviraj Singh Deo then became the ruler of Patna State. Maharaja Prithvi Raj Singh Deo upgraded the English school to a high school in 1906, and it was called Prithvi Raj High School or PR High School.

My younger maternal uncle, Bhikari Charan Panigrahi, had come to Balangir to complete his high school at PR High School in the 1930s, and he went back to Surangi to serve under the Raja of Surangi. My eldest brother, Koramoni Panigrahi, followed my uncle to come to Balangir to study at PR High School. After graduating from high school, he worked in Balangir as a clerk and a teacher for a few years and then started the wholesale fruits and betel business. He would regularly get crates of betel leaves from south Odisha and distribute them to the merchants in Balangir and the surrounding areas. He would also get bananas and mangoes from Andhra Pradesh coastal areas by train wagons and trucks and distribute them. His business had prospered, and he had become a prominent businessman in Balangir. When I came to Balangir in 1953 to study, the family was residing in a large double-storied house with an attached garden in Rugudipara.

LP School

Right next to Prithvi Raj High School, on the other side of the road, the Lower Primary School (LP School) was located, and there were classes from kindergarten (Shishu) to grade 3 there. I was admitted to this LP School in grade 3. This was the premier LP School in the town. My uncle's eldest son, Prafulla, was already admitted as a student at this school since grade 2.

We had to get ready by 10 AM and walk to the LP School, which was more than one km from the house in Ragudipara. We would have a fast lunch with whatever was already cooked by that time, and then walk toward the school. On the way, we crossed the main chowk on the road that came from the bus stand and went towards Titlagarh, the train station on the western end of the district. We would walk toward the main town, and on the way, see the Additional District Magistrate's quarters on the left. There were quarters for the policemen. The police headquarters was at the far end of this lane. Facing the police headquarters was the main courthouse of the district on the other side of the road. We would then walk through the main bus stand of the town. Both sides of the road were lined up with different shops, restaurants, fruit stalls, and stationery shops. We would then walk on the side of Narsingh Pond.

Adjoining it were Karangakata Pond and Marwari Pond. The LP school was on the side of the last two ponds. The school had ample playgrounds on the side, and there was a garden for raising vegetables and flowers. I was very excited to be studying at the LP school. Although I had never used a pencil and had never written anything in a notebook, and all of my writing was on a slate in the village school, I had no difficulty adjusting to the new environment. In those days, we wrote using ink with a special pen fitted with a nib, which was often dipped in the inkpot during the writing period. The use of a fountain pen instead of the pen and the inkpot was also introduced in the schools at the time. I did not have any trouble in the mathematics class since I knew the multiplication table by heart up to 25. The only other subjects were literature, Odia language, and writing. I had no problem here, since I knew and spoke almost chaste Odia with an accent that was akin to the people from the Ganjam district. The spoken language at home and outside in Balangir was in Sambalpuri, a dialect of the Odia language. There were quite a few words from Hindi in Sambalpuri, and it also sounded like Bengali, partly because of the verb endings sounding similar to Bengali. I was able to speak and communicate in Sambalpuri in just a few days. The fact that I could also speak chaste Odia without any effort, because of my background in the Ganjam district, was an advantage in reading and writing in the government schools in Balangir.

The LP school in Balangir was a boys' school. However, there were two girls in the third grade, one being the daughter of the Principal of the Sanskrit college, which was across the street next to PR High School, and the other girl was the daughter of the jailer of the district jail, which was four blocks away. I remember playing and talking with Shashi, the principal's daughter, as she was waiting for her father to finish his work. I never saw them again after the school year, since the girls joined a Government Girls' High School, which was a block away from PR High School. I topped the class in both the half-yearly and the final examinations. Hence, I had a very successful start in the education arena in Balangir.

After the school year, I visited my ancestral village so that a sacred thread ceremony could be performed on me. It was an elaborate set of affairs at the back of our house in the village. I wore a short dhoti made out of a set of thick strings similar to a forest product from the tree bark. At the end of all the chanting of the hymns in Sanskrit in front of the holy fire rejuvenated with pure ghee, I went to the sandy riverside along with some of the relatives and onlookers. I acted as if I wanted to run away from the village to become a hermit. At that point, my maternal uncle held me back and convinced me to stay in society. At any rate, I was ready now to take up bigger responsibilities on the path towards a householder life. At the age of nine, I had my six-strand sacred thread wrapped around my shoulder and belly. Henceforth, I had to show proper respect to the sacred thread and observe proper etiquette during daily affairs.

PR High School

I came back to Balangir a few weeks after my thread ceremony. I obtained admission into Prithvi Raj High School (PR High School) in June 1954, at the opening of the school after the summer vacation. In the fourth and fifth grades, there was only one section of about forty-five students. In the sixth and seventh grades, there was one additional section each to allow students from the upper primary schools in the town to join the school.

Almost half of my classmates from the LP school were enrolled in the fourth grade of PR High School. So, I had good company and was on familiar grounds. At that time, all the subjects were taught in Odia in the fourth and fifth grades. We had arithmetic, literature, health and hygiene, geography, history, and drawing as subjects in the two grades. I used to top in all of the subjects except drawing and had overall stood first in the half-yearly and yearly examinations in both grades.

Starting with sixth grade, we had an additional section in the class, and about fifty new students joined the class, including some in our original section. We had classes in three additional languages: English, Sanskrit, and Hindi. Hindi continued up to grade 8, but the other two continued until the 11th grade, the final year of the school at that time. In the sixth and seventh grades, the other additional subjects were geometry, including mensuration and crafts, specifically tailoring of banians and shorts. As usual, I had topped the overall class in the half-yearly and yearly examinations in the sixth grade. I had also topped in the half-yearly in the seventh grade among all the students in both sections.

In January 1958, while I was pursuing the second half of the academic year, we got a telegram from our ancestral village that my father had suddenly expired in the village. In those days, there were no telephones in the houses. We had received a letter from my father only a few weeks earlier, and he seemed to be alright and had rather written about my mother having some health problems at the time. So, his end came suddenly. He was perhaps down with heart failure or stroke and died a few hours thereafter. He was only sixty-five years old at the time.

Once we got the bad news, my elder brothers arranged to rent a special car from the State Transport Corporation with a driver so that the family could travel by road and reach the village as soon as possible. Going by train through Vizianagaram and Icchapuram in Andhra Pradesh would take at least one and a half or two days. We all traveled by car through the fair-weather road passing through Boudh to Berhampur. Unfortunately, the car had a breakdown near Bhanjanagar, at the Kalinga Mountain hills crossings. We finally reached Berhampur by taking a ride on a government bus. From there, we traveled by bus to Patrapur via Icchapuram. We had to walk about one km through the fields to arrive in our village the next evening.

The shraddha ceremony for my father continued until the tenth day after his death. From the seventh day onward, there were feasts every evening for about five hundred people that also included Brahmins from the surrounding villages. The feast on the tenth day was the most elaborate. We, all four brothers, had to shave our heads and then bathe in the river. After the fifteenth day of my father's death, we took the train from Icchapuram to go back to Balangir. My mother stayed in the village in our ancestral house along with my third brother and his wife, and they were now responsible for taking care of all the affairs relating to farming in the village.

I came back to Balangir and joined the school after more than two weeks of absence. That year, I did not have to take the yearly examination arranged by the school. Instead, I was asked to take the seventh-grade board examination being held at our school. Top students from the seventh grade of all the schools in the district appeared for this examination. As a result of this examination, selected students were given a monthly stipend of Rs 15 every month for the next four years until the completion of high school. I was notified to be one of the recipients of this monthly scholarship given by the state government.

With the start of the eighth grade, we started to cover the syllabus designed for the matriculation examination of the eleventh grade. General Science included physics, chemistry, botany, zoology, hygiene, astronomy, geology, etc. The mathematics syllabus included algebra, arithmetic, geometry, and mensuration. The social studies syllabus included the historical and geographical aspects of different societies in the world and India, in particular detail. The English syllabus consisted of two papers, the first one on the selected prose and poetry texts, and the second one on selected books of stories and social institutions, plus the writing of essays and papers. We also had a compulsory paper on Odia and another on Sanskrit. My chosen optional mathematics paper included trigonometry, algebra, and geometry. We were not taught Hindi beyond the eighth grade. However, I had on the side prepared and appeared for Rastrabhasha examinations conducted from Wardha and had passed Prarambhik, Pravesh, and Parichaya levels in Hindi while studying in seventh and eighth grades in high school.

We were moved to the room right next to the science laboratories, and different science experiments could be demonstrated more easily during the science classes. There was an additional section in the classes starting from the eighth grade, and this allowed students from different middle schools and other high schools to study in this special government high school of the district. There were now about one hundred and forty students enrolled in the three sections of the class. As before, I topped in both the half-yearly and the yearly examinations among all the students in the class.

The summer vacation after the completion of the eighth grade was very special because of the activities associated with the locality where our house was located in Rugudipara. There was a small primary school and open fields in front of our house. Working with the students and professionals of the locality, I set up a library in one of the rooms of the school. It was named Gangadhar Meher Sahitya Samiti in the name of the most well-known poet of western Odisha. We also secured the grant of a radio from the public information department of the government so that members can listen to the radio during weekends and holidays. There used to be games of soccer, volleyball, badminton, and cricket in the adjoining fields.

The group decided that a selected two-hour Odia play would be practiced by the group during the summer. It was to be staged in Patnagarh, the original capital and fort of the Patna state. Patnagarh was a smaller town compared to Balangir and had the district block headquarters building. It was not unusual in those days for drama groups from Balangir to go to smaller towns to provide them the entertainment and raise some funds for the organization. We practiced for about four weeks and then went to Patnagarh to stage the play. I had a small part in it, where I acted as the young boy who grew up to become the hero of the play. In those days, the female roles were also being played by males. We went to Patnagarh and prepared the stage and audience areas around an open stage building that was there in Patnagarh. It was a smaller version of the large 'Kalamandala' (Art House) building in Balangir. We advertised in the town and sold tickets for the play. We staged the play for two days and then came back to

Balangir with the troop in a small truck. This was an exciting experience, both in terms of practice during the month before the play and the actual staging in an unknown town.

There was a strong focus on studying during the final three years of high school. The statewide matriculation examination was being conducted by the Odisha High School Certificate (HSC) Board for the students of the eleventh grade who were allowed to appear for this examination towards the end of the academic session. The HSC examination covered material taught in all three years, plus materials covered in general science, social studies, and mathematics from the eighth grade. I had chosen mathematics as my optional subject, similar to what many of the top students had done. So, the optional mathematics covered trigonometry, geometry, and algebra. I also took special mathematics and Sanskrit tuition classes during the tenth and eleventh grades. I had always topped all the school examinations during this period. But our goal was to rank within the 'Best Ten' of all the candidates in the State.

There were regular cultural functions in the school, especially for the Ganesh Chaturthi in the Aug/Sept time frame and Saraswati Panchami in the Jan/Feb time frame. Each class used to put up short plays and other entertainment programs during those evenings at the school premises. Each section of the class also produced a handwritten book in Jan/Feb that had stories, poems, and essays in Odia, English, and Hindi. We had different debating competitions, primarily in Odia, but sometimes in Hindi and English. At the annual school day festivals, different short plays, songs, and skits were practiced and then staged with the supervision of one of the members of the teaching staff. I especially remember delivering a five-minute speech while acting as the revolutionary Udham Singh during one of the annual day celebrations.

The school provided plenty of opportunities for taking up cultural and sports activities through different competitions. I had only been able to advance in the game of badminton to the top rungs in high school. I mainly played other games in the localities around our house to spend the weekends and the late afternoons, but I was not good enough or was not interested in getting into any sports teams in the school or outside in the town. The game of badminton allowed us to play in the evenings too, under the light, and hence was convenient and limited to playing with a few friends.

In the cultural area, we had regular weekly debating societies to debate in Odia, Hindi, and English. A school magazine was published every year around the time of Saraswati Puja, with a senior teaching staff advising in this effort. In the tenth grade, I was chosen as the literary secretary of the school and hence assisted in the publication of the magazine called Parijata. I did write poems and short stories in Odia and essays in English.

There was participation from the high school students in the town-wide competitions held by different cultural and government organizations. I participated in most of these debating and writing competitions, and especially remember getting the best prize for essays in English in the townwide competitions.

The eleventh grade was largely spent focusing on the preparation for the final matriculation examination to be conducted statewide in March 1962. I was taking special tuition for mathematics and Sanskrit. We did have a welcome break for two weeks when we visited Kolkata as part of an excursion trip led by a teacher. About ten of us were on this trip to explore Kolkata. We stayed in a rental building adjacent to Purabi Cinema Hall and visited the tourist attractions, such as the Victoria Memorial, Botanical Garden, Khidirpur Zoo, Birla Industrial Museum, Dakshineshwar Temple, Kolkata Museum, and movie studios. It certainly enlarged our general outlook. On the way back, we stayed in the new steel town of Rourkela in Odisha and saw the steel plant that was set up with the help of engineers from Germany.

I had topped the class overall in the final school examination conducted in December, just before the statewide High School Certificate (HSC) examination. The results of the HSC examination came out in May timeframe and unfortunately, I was not among the top ten students in the state. I scored the highest overall in PR High School and scored 93 in General Science, and full marks in mathematics and optional mathematics. But I got the highest marks in Social Studies in the School, and it was only around 60. Similarly, the scores for the language papers were in the sixties, except for Sanskrit, where I scored in the seventies. The marks received varied a lot depending on where the answer books were sent for grading and the yardstick used by the grader. In any case, the high school chapter was finished. Although I did not come out in the top ten in the HSC examination, it was somewhere in the top 25 or so. We did not find out the actual ranking.

That summer vacation after the HSC examination, I visited my village and spent a couple of weeks there. I also spent a couple of weeks with my uncle's sons. They also had appeared for the HSC examination and were of the same age. Their parents were talking about getting them married after a year and were looking for candidates of nine to eleven years of age from among the Brahmin girls in the villages around. The whole area was still following the child marriage custom, especially for the girls. It so happened that both of my cousin brothers, one six months younger and the other one year older than me, got married the following spring while they were in the first year of college, studying pre-university science in Berhampur. Of course, the consummation of marriage would be in a few years, only when the bride is ready after puberty. But the choice is made for the couples while all of them are still too young to discover and choose.

I came back to Balangir after the vacation in the village and concentrated on the next course of action. I was interested in studying either the pre-university science or the pre-university arts streams. One of the goals at that time was to appear for the Indian Administrative Service (IAS) examination, and in that regard, it was beneficial at the time to join the arts stream. However, I spent many hours consulting with my close friend Surendra Purohit. He had decided to join the arts stream and would later go for post-graduate studies in Political Science and appear for the IAS examinations. I decided to join the science stream, considering that I had scored so well in the science and mathematics subjects. It was also considered a good track for IAS, where one changes after one year of pre-university science. I applied to Ravenshaw College, the pre-eminent college in Odisha, and was accepted to pursue pre-university science with economics as the fourth optional subject. However, the pre-university science stream with biology as the fourth optional subject was started that year at the local college in Balangir, the Rajendra College. So, I decided to join Rajendra College, especially since that allowed me to stay at home rather than staying at the college hostel, as it would have been if I had joined Ravenshaw College.

Rajendra College

Rajendra College was started in the year 1943 by the erstwhile ruler of Patna State, Maharaja Rajendra Narayan Singh Deo, the adopted son of Maharaja Prithvi Raj Singh. It was a college offering arts streams up to the Bachelor of Arts (BA) level and commerce streams up to the intermediate level. The science stream was started only in 1961, when a new wing of the college was introduced for the purpose. For the entrants in the year 1962, a pre-university science stream was offered with physics, chemistry, mathematics, and biology as the optional subjects. I was admitted in July 1962 into the pre-university science stream with physics, chemistry, and mathematics as my optional subjects, and the fourth optional subject of biology.

There were about eighty students in the pre-university science stream that year, and they came from all over the district, especially from the sub-divisional headquarters towns, such as Patnagarh, Titlagarh, and Sonepur, in addition to Balangir. All our classes were held in the Science Wing, which was newly constructed and was also equipped with the new laboratories of the physics, chemistry, and biology departments.

After the start of the classes, there was an election campaign for the new office bearers for the college union for the new year. I was persuaded by many of my friends, especially the ones coming from PR High School, to contest for the post of Assistant General Secretary of the Union. Though I had just joined the college, I had the advantage of being local to Balangir. My opponent was from Titlagarh, but he had the advantage of being in the second year of the arts stream. There was canvassing for the votes for about two weeks, and it culminated in the election speech on the election day in the college. As the counting of votes continued, the votes for me were way ahead, and my opponent was sure of losing the election and ran away to a village close by. In the final count, I lost the election by two votes. My opponent had a more extensive campaign and support at all ends, since his elder brother was running for the President of the union at the same time. Nonetheless, it was an interesting start to my college career.

The academic calendar started smoothly in the college. In addition to the four science optional subjects (physics, chemistry, mathematics, and biology), we had English, Odia, and General Knowledge as the subject papers for the university examination to be conducted at the end of the academic session. Since we had studied science subjects in Odia in high school, we had to get used to the new terminology in English. That was the problem for most of the students. I had no difficulty in any of the subjects, and I stood first overall in the college examinations conducted. The university examinations were held in March / April 1963, and then I went to Hirakud to appear for the IIT Entrance examination. From there, I went to the village directly.

The results of the pre-university science examination came out after about two months, and to my surprise and joy, I had stood second in the rank out of all the candidates passing that examination in Odisha. Although I could not achieve the top rank in the previous year in the matriculation examination, my achievement in the pre-university science examination was very satisfying. Later on, I found that I had two marks less than the first rank holder, and it was because he had about ten marks more in biology. I remember I had not done well in the frog dissection part of the biology practical examination in the final, because the frog given to me was too small!

Standing second in the university examination ensured that I got a monthly scholarship of Rs75/ every month until the completion of the Bachelor's degree. Finally, I got a call from IIT Kharagpur to come for the reselection interview. I went there and asked for a seat in Electronics and Electrical Communication Engineering since I had developed a strong interest in that area by being exposed to radio and marveling at all the technology associated with the transmission and reception of radio signals. Television had not come to India and Odisha at that time, but we had heard about it too. The selection head in the interview session told me that there were no more seats available in Electronics and Electrical Communication Engineering. However, they recommended that I join the Physics program at IIT, which covers Electronics to a large extent. I agreed to enlist in the B. Science (Physics) program at IIT Kharagpur.

I took the train from Kharagpur to Bhubaneswar to get my final marksheet in the university examination, so that I could apply for entrance into other places besides IIT. I had not applied anywhere else besides taking the IIT entrance examination. It dawned on me after coming out of Kharagpur that I should not join the physics program in an engineering school like IIT, especially since my goal was not to perform research on basic sciences, but to apply technology for the benefit of Indian society. This thought solidified when I met on the train another candidate who was returning from the interview at IIT Kharagpur. He was the person who had obtained the first rank in the pre-university science examination by securing two more marks. He was returning disappointed, since he did not get the branch of engineering he wanted at IIT.

After coming back to Balangir, I found that my

friend Omprakash, who stood seventh in the University examination and was from Rajendra College and Prithvi Raj High School earlier, also returned from IIT Kharagpur disappointed. Both of us decided to go directly to Rourkela with our academic documents and apply for admission at the Regional Engineering College (REC) – Rourkela, which had started functioning a couple of years earlier. We went to the college office and obtained the application forms, and submitted them with all the required documents. Since both of us had scored so high in our university examinations, we were assured of getting admission into the engineering program. The selection of the branch of engineering was to occur at the beginning of the third year of the five-year course at REC. Hence, there was no problem of getting whatever branch we would then desire. So, we got selected by REC-Rourkela and were admitted there, starting the classes in July 1963. Thus, my studying career in Balangir came to an end after joining REC-Rourkela. Thereafter, I would visit Balangir during all college vacations since that's where my main roots were planted by that time. In addition to the members of my brothers' families, I had a large number of friends associated right from primary school to high school and college. There were also friends from the Rugudipara locality where our family lived. Balangir was the only town in Odisha that I knew thoroughly, having studied there for ten years and staying there since the age of eight. Hence, that is always my town!

3. NIT and IIT World

NIT Rourkela

I joined the Regional Engineering College (REC), now renamed as National Institute of Technology (NIT), located in the steel city of Rourkela, Odisha, in the first year of the five-year engineering program of the academic session 1963-1964. REC Rourkela started only two years earlier and was the second engineering college in the state of Odisha, the University College of Engineering at Burla, Sambalpur, being the first engineering college operating for a while.

There were about one hundred fifty students in the first year of the engineering program in July 1963. Of these, half of the students were from various parts of Odisha, and the other half were from various other parts of India. There was a special contingent of about ten students from Assam that year. There was excitement in the air since the college was relatively new and the department buildings were being constructed. I stayed in Hostel 1, which was nearest to the college and accommodated all of the first and second-year students who took admission that year. I stayed with my friend Omprakash in a room on the second floor, along with two other students, Maheshwar Sahoo and Dipen Das from Balasore in Odisha. For about a month, there was mass ragging in the evenings by senior students from the other hostel nearby. We somehow managed to survive through all that.

Professor Bhubaneswar Behera, the Principal, welcomed us in a special address and told us that engineering was a noble profession in the service of society. The engineers build and maintain roads, dams, houses, buildings, plants, and factories. He related some of his experiences during the construction of the Hirakud dam on the river Mahanadi. That was one of the first large-scale hydroelectric projects in India after independence. We felt proud to have joined the engineering program at a national institute of repute.

The first-year engineering program included papers in physics, chemistry, mathematics, and English, besides the engineering subjects, such as surveying, machine drawing, etc.

Our hostel was about half a kilometer from Bandhamunda Hills, and we could see the stretch of barren land dotted with small trees up to the hills. The cafeteria provided at the hostel did not always have good meals. Hence, fifty of the students joined a vegetarian mess that was started in a small building behind the hostel. So, I was a vegetarian for most of that year since both Omprakash and I joined this special vegetarian mess for the meals.

There were riots that winter in East Pakistan, and there was a rumor of Hindus being killed, and the train compartments were bringing dead and wounded people from there. Rourkela was a new city built after independence, and had a significant portion of its working population from East Bengal and West Punjab, who had migrated and settled down in Rourkela as jobs became available in the steel plant. Some anti-social elements from these groups of people started a riotous atmosphere in the steel town to take revenge against the Muslim population that had also settled down around Rourkela and the surrounding areas. The college was closed for a few days and was sealed, so that there would be no one moving in or out of the campus.

One night, we heard the sound of some people screaming in the fields in front of our hostel. The next morning, we saw the bodies of some people scattered around that area. The situation finally got better when the military was called to take control of the situation. It was my first and only experience of the Hindu-Muslim riot situation. In Balangir, there were only a small number of Muslim families, and there were only one or two classmates who had surnames associated with the Muslim religion. They were just part of the urban society in Balangir, and I had no experience of serious differences.

The academic calendar went very smoothly. I was excited to take part in all the new engineering workshops and drawing classes. I was also chosen as one of the two class representatives and participated in the cultural competitions and shows for the college day. Overall, I stood first amongst all the first-year engineering students in both the half-yearly and final examinations that were conducted by the college. The university examination was held thereafter for all the students in the two engineering colleges of Utkal University: REC Rourkela and Engineering College at Burla.

There was then a notification in the papers for admission into the second year of engineering in the IITs. Both Omprakash and I responded to that and appeared for the entrance examination held at Hirakud, Sambalpur. As a result, I was called for an interview at IIT Kharagpur, and I obtained admission into the second year of Electronics and Electrical Communication Engineering. Thus, my goal to study at IIT Kharagpur in Electronics was finally achieved. After joining the classes at IIT Kharagpur in July for two weeks, I came to REC Rourkela to seek my transfer certificate and get my marksheet in the last university examination. The Principal, Professor Behera, did not give me the transfer certificate, but no one asked for one at IIT Kharagpur, and hence there was no problem. I found that I had stood second in the university examination, and another student of REC Rourkela had stood first in that examination. I was especially surprised to find that I had scored only a forty-five percent mark in the English paper. I had always scored at the highest level in the college-level examinations in English. It seemed the teacher who graded my paper did not like my writing of very long explanations. That was my lowest score ever in a paper, and I learned the lesson to be brief and very much to the point in future writings.

Although I spent only one year at NIT Rourkela, it was a memorable year. I learned a lot about general engineering besides going through a thorough grounding in physics, chemistry, and mathematics. I formed a deep bond of friendship with many of my classmates there. Seven of us had taken a trip together to Bombay during the Durga Puja vacation to explore that metropolis for ourselves. We stayed at Dadar after arriving by train from Rourkela. We saw Elephanta Caves, Kamla Nehru Park, Arey Milk Colony, Borivali National Park, Juhu Beach, Nariman Point, and Chowpatty area. This friendship with NIT friends was renewed when I lived later in Bhubaneswar, since scores of them lived there, and Bhubaneswar was the focus city for all of the activities of the NIT Alumni Association.

IIT Kharagpur

Indian Institute of Technology (IIT), Kharagpur, was the first of many IITs to be established in India after independence. The classes started in the Hijli Jail building in 1954. When I joined IIT in July 1964, it was the only one amongst the five IITs (IIT Kharagpur, IIT Bombay, IIT Madras, IIT Delhi, and IIT Kanpur) that had Electronics and Electrical Communication Engineering as a separate branch apart from Electrical Engineering. So, I was very happy to be able to join the program at IIT Kharagpur.

There were only about fifty students who were admitted to the second year of the five-year program. They came from all over India, and most of them came after a Bachelor's degree in science. All of us were put into one section and had all our classes together, although we belonged to different assigned branches. There were only three of us in this group who were assigned the Electronics stream: Anand Vaidya from Goa and Satyapriya Majumdar from Mumbai, besides me. My friend Mohammed Salikuddin from Odisha was part of this batch too and had joined after a BSc degree in Physics.

I was assigned Azad Hall of Residence, one of the original three Halls of Residence, the others being Nehru Hall and Patel Hall. All three residence halls were the farthest from the IIT main building, and we used a bicycle to travel the distance. The ragging period of the first two weeks was beneficial in learning from the seniors living in the same hostel. The IIT hostels were not segregated by seniority, and students from all five years lived in the same hostel and benefited from the experience of the seniors. New students shared a room with another roommate, and after the first year in the hostel, everyone had a single room assigned.

The classes for the newly admitted second-year students were held together for all the subjects. Besides physics, chemistry, and mathematics, other subjects were English, Industrial Development, Drawing, Surveying, etc.

The first trimester went very fast. I got a first division

as far as the total marks were concerned, and did not achieve the level I had wanted. I realized that I had not done proper preparation to achieve the best. During the second trimester, I did better planning and preparation for the subjects, and the results from the second trimester examinations were excellent. I had stood first amongst all the second-year new students in the total marks. Although I worked the same number of hours, I kept my aim high with full concentration. That made the difference. In the final trimester of the year. I achieved good results, such that I achieved the first rank amongst all the students of Electronics and Electrical Communication Engineering for the year, amongst both new and old students who had joined a year earlier in 1963. I was very happy with this overall performance at IIT Kharagpur and visited homes in the village and Balangir during the summer vacation.

The other exciting event of the following academic year was the 1965 war between India and Pakistan that happened in August-September. Since the Kalai Kunda airbase was near Kharagpur, we saw a dogfight between the planes in the middle of the day, and one of the enemy planes went down and crashed on the outskirts. This was part of an attack by the government of East Pakistan. There was no further incident, and the war ended with a ceasefire agreement between the two nations.

The third year of the Electronics and Electrical Communication Engineering started, and all the classes were held along with the students of the Electronics stream. There were twenty-five total students in our stream. The subjects that year were all related to engineering, such as mechanics, fluid dynamics, electrical circuits, and laboratory. We also had economics as a subject. There was only one subject in electronics and a laboratory in the third year.

I stood first overall in all three trimester examinations held in the third year. I came back to Balangir during the summer vacation. As part of practical training, I visited the local electrical office that generated DC and AC power and distributed power in Balangir town.

The program of the fourth year was very much focused on Electronics and Electrical Communication Engineering. We also had a paper that covered general and abnormal psychology and industrial psychology. This was the toughest year for the electronics students, and about twenty-five percent of the students did not get a class promotion to the final year of the program. I liked all the subjects and maintained the top position in the class in all the trimester examinations.

After the completion of the final trimester in the fourth year, I went to Bengaluru to take industrial training at Bharat Electronics Ltd. During the summer of 1967, Bharat Electronics was the only electronics organization at the time in India designing, developing, and manufacturing electronic systems and devices. We spent one week each in their selected departments and laboratories. I specifically remember now being in the semiconductor laboratory where they were dealing with germanium and silicon ingots. There was the radar department developing many products for the government. There was the communication department developing a walkie-talkie and other signaling systems for the army. The microwave department had many of the special devices required in communication applications.

I stayed in the YMCA quarters adjoining Caban Park and took the B.E.L. buses from around there in the morning to the company site and then back at the end of the day. Bengaluru was a very nice, quiet, and green city then, and

I remember sipping drinks in the Three Aces restaurant on MG Road and elsewhere along with a friend from a Jabalpur engineering college. I went to Mysore by bus on one of the weekends to see Brindavan Gardens near there, with my classmate from IIT, Pratul Ajmera. Overall, it was a pleasant summer, and I returned to Kharagpur by train, stopping on the way at Pithapuram in Andhra Pradesh to visit my second brother's family and then stopping at Icchapuram to visit Bodoboranga.

Final year classes started when students who had failed and were from senior batches joined our class. In addition to the electronics subjects, we also had operations research, statistics, quantum mechanics, and Indian philosophy during the year. We had to select a graduation project at the beginning of the year and had to complete that during the year, and then submit a project report at the end of the year. I selected a project in the line communication laboratory, which consisted of building the circuits relating to a one-digit hybrid pulse code modulation system.

During the second trimester, we had a field trip to the Delhi area to visit some of the Landmark laboratories there. We visited the National Physical Laboratories in Delhi. I also managed to slip away from the Delhi area and visited the Taj Mahal and Agra Fort in Agra and Akbar's Court building at Fatehpur Sikri.

During the year, I visited Calcutta to take the Graduate Records Examination (GRE) in Kolkata so that I could apply to American and Canadian universities for graduate study. I applied to several universities and received offers of research assistantships from many universities. I was also offered a two-year fellowship at the University of Illinois, Urbana-Champaign. I was also offered admission to Stanford University. I was offered research assistantships from the University of Rochester in New York and the University of Waterloo in Canada. I decided to accept the fellowship offer from the University of Illinois since it had one of the top five graduate schools in Electrical Engineering in America, and previous toppers in Electronics from IIT Kharagpur had gone there to pursue graduate study.

IIT Campus Life

During my first year of stay in the hostel at IIT, I shared a room with Anand Vaidya from Panjim, Goa, at Azad Hall during the 1964 – 1965 academic year. Since Goa was just recently liberated from the Portuguese occupation, Anand related to us stories of life there. I remember going with him to the Kalei Kunda airbase to meet one of his relatives there. He was also very active in the activities of the Radio Club, and I had accompanied him to the club premises a few times.

In the subsequent three years of my stay in Azad Hall, my room was in different wings along with my batch of students from Kolkata: Ambar Sarkar from Electronics, Arup Paul and Lalit Nanda from Chemical, Prithviraj Sen and Pulak Dutta from Mechanical, and Debasis Sengupta from Civil. During the final year, just before getting dispersed, we had dinner outings with this group of friends. Soumen Bandopadhyay and Purnendu Chatterjee used to visit our wing too often. Vasan Raman and D. K. Sharma were two batchmates from Electronics who also resided in Azad Hall, and they were my laboratory partners.

There were many from junior batches in Azad Hall with whom I had friendly relations, Arvind Jain from Mechanical, Panda from Metallurgy, and many others. Since Nehru Hall was next to Azad, Ramamurthy, and

Satyapriya from Nehru Hall often came. Salikuddin from LR Hall came many times during the Hall Day celebrations. There was an informal association of students and staff from Odisha at IIT. It used to hold annual picnics. The teaching staff participating in these activities were, Head of Mining, Professor Mishra, and his singer wife, Minati Mishra, Professor B.K. Saraf from Electronics, Professor Duryodhan Mangaraj from Chemistry, etc.

Whatever time was there after the study time, I relaxed by taking care of my health. I made sure that I got eight hours of sleep every night. I often bought special fruits available after lunchtime and arranged to get a glass of hot milk in the evening every day. The short stroll on the road after the early dinners before 7.30 PM was my favorite. Unfortunately, there was not much scope for playing games since I was only good at the game of badminton and had played a few times in Azad Hall. I was never much interested in NCC activities, although it became compulsory for every college student after the India-China war in 1962. I continued performing yogic exercises since my high school days to keep myself strong and fit. There was no scope for swimming activities on the campus. That is something I had developed a liking for in Balangir, where I swam in the biggest pond in the town close to our residence.

During the final trimester of the final year, I took a trip to the Puri and Bhubaneswar areas along with several of my electronics classmates so that they could see the main attractions of Odisha before they finished their studies at IIT and went home to the distant cities and towns. I had also not been to this part of Odisha, except for a quick train trip to Bhubaneswar in 1963 to get the marksheet from the Pre-University examination. Satyapriya Majumdar and Ramamurthy, both from Mumbai, came along with D.K.

Sharma from Delhi. We stayed at a hotel on the beach in Puri for a couple of days and went to see the Konark temple. We also saw the Bhubaneswar and Cuttack areas.

I completed the graduation project on a 'Uni-digit Hybrid Pulse Code Modulation System' and submitted a copy of the report to the Department of Electronics and Electrical Communication Engineering. I went through the final year viva-voce examination at the end of the year. Overall, I stood first in all three of the trimester examinations.

The four years that I spent in Kharagpur established a solid foundation in my professional career. The teaching staff in the Department of Electronics was very cordial, and the years passed by quickly without any problem. It was finally time to bid goodbye to IIT Kharagpur. I gave away my cycle to the person from the kitchen staff who used to give me a glass of hot milk every night. I gathered all my other stuff and took the train to Balangir from Kharagpur station.

4. University of Illinois

Travel to America

As part of the travel package to the United States, we had the flight from Kolkata to Athens, Greece, through Japan Airlines. Omprakash and I were given a farewell at the airport by Omprakash's relatives, who had come from Odisha, and my relatives and friends. I had only eight dollars in my pocket since that was all that I was allowed at the time. However, Omprakash had a lot more dollars with him since he was joining the University of Iowa, Ames, for graduate studies in Electrical Engineering with his funds. But, both of us were allowed free room and board for one day at the hotel as part of the travel package.

We saw the temple of the goddess Parthenon in Athens and had the opportunity to see the city of Athens on a bright September afternoon. We had a quiet dinner at the hotel, and we had to take off the next morning from Athens to go to Frankfurt in West Germany, flying with British Overseas Airways Corporation (BOAC). I spent a day in Frankfurt visiting the markets there and used a few dollars to buy a shirt as a memento. The next day, we took the flight to London with BOAC. We were similarly given room and board at a hotel in London. We roamed around London the next day, going around the Thames, walking over the London Bridge. We visited the British Parliament building, Buckingham Palace, and Trafalgar Square. We reached the airport in the evening to take the flight from

Heathrow to O'Hare airport in Chicago, again flying with BOAC.

We were aboard the flight, and the plane flew for about an hour and was over the Atlantic. We were then told that one of the engines of the aircraft had failed, and hence the plane had to go back to Heathrow rather than take a chance to cross the Atlantic Ocean and fly to Chicago. We flew back to Heathrow and were informed of a later flight, scheduled with another aircraft. We had to inform Sam Pitroda in Chicago, who was supposed to pick us up at O'Hare and host us for the night at his residence in Chicago. Omprakash's family knew Pitroda's family in Titlagarh and had arranged this so that it was smooth for both of us in Chicago before flying to our ultimate destinations in Illinois and Iowa.

Sam Pitroda picked us up when the rescheduled flight arrived in Chicago, and we spent the night at his residence. The next morning, Sam Pitroda first dropped his wife off at her work and then dropped us off at the airport terminal. My friend Omprakash flew from O'Hare to Ames, Iowa. I flew to Champaign, flying with Ozark Airlines. There was a van waiting for me at the airport, and that dropped me off at Sherman Hall of Residence at the University of Illinois, Urbana-Champaign campus.

Life on the American Campus

Sherman Hall was a graduate hall of residence and five blocks away from the Electrical Engineering building, where I had most of my classes. I stayed in Sherman Hall for the first semester and then moved to Daniels Hall for the next semester, since it was more convenient to walk to classes and for meals at Illini Residence Halls. During the first summer of 1969, I moved to an apartment that I shared with two other students. That summer was remarkable because the astronauts landed on the moon for the first time. There was a shared kitchen, and we prepared food there or ate out. After the summer, I took a two-bedroom apartment on lease along with Prakash Shingi, who was pursuing his doctorate in social sciences. During this time, I tried cooking in the apartment, but never liked it, and ended up eating most days in the Union Cafeteria.

I moved back to Daniels Hall beginning Fall of 1970 and enrolled in the cafeteria in the Illini Hall across the street for regular meals. For the next two years, I stayed here and worked at the Digital Computer Laboratory, which was two blocks away. In early 1971, I purchased a second-hand car, a General Motors Thunderbird, and that gave me more freedom. My friend Sanak Mishra also purchased a similar car, and we used to go for dinner together many times on Sunday nights to have pizza and beer, since I did not have dinner the Sunday nights at Illini Hall.

We had regular cultural events and Indian movies. I participated in most of these and other cultural activities for foreign and American students. The Sunday movie at the auditorium in the Quad was a favorite. I was friendly with many Indian students who were enrolled in Electrical Engineering and Computer Science like me: Yogendra Singh, Mehrnosh Cooper, Shiv Verma, Kanti Jain, Debasish Bose, etc. I had friendly relations with many from other departments: Subhransu Chakravarthy, Anup Mukhopadhyay, and Prafulla Panigrahi from Metallurgy. Don Parsons from the Toronto area was a friend right from the beginning when he was in many of my classes.

I was close to many other students during the 1970 to 1972 period: Murli Pahoja, who became President of the Indian Students Association, Upendra Kachru, who joined the university at this time for an MBA program, Asha Bhalaria, who came from Kolkata to complete a Master's in Architecture, and Virginia, the nutritionist from Chicago, and many others from Africa, Latin America and Asia. Bernard Tse from Hong Kong was a roommate in the computer laboratory and was one of the first ones to later start a company along with his wife to make a line of 'Wyse' computer terminals. Hats off to Bernie for his entrepreneurship and being one of the first multi-millionaires! Trevor Mudge from Scotland was another friend in the computer lab who later became a professor of computer science.

We also had exposure to a few American host families. I remember visiting the Nickels in Springfield, Illinois, for a few days during my first Christmas break in 1968. I visited another American family in Clinton, a town close to Urbana, who dropped me off at Daniels Hall after the visit to their town in 1970. I especially remember visiting the mobile home of a fellow graduate student and his family during the first Thanksgiving break in November 1968, when his young son was surprised to meet an Indian, whereas he expected to meet an American Indian!

Master's Program

With a fellowship awarded by the University of Illinois for two years, I was free to take the full load of graduate courses toward the Master's and Doctoral degrees, and I did not have to render any services, teaching, or research. So, I enrolled in four required graduate courses in the 1968 fall session and secured A grades in all four graduate courses at the end of the semester. I enrolled in four more courses in the winter semester, and since that filled up the course requirements toward the master's degree, I was required to take the qualifying examination towards the PhD degree early in that semester. I passed the qualifying examination and was all set to start the doctoral program in a chosen area.

I was awarded a quarter-time assistantship to work in the Electromagnetics laboratory. However, I did not want to pursue that because my interest was not in that area, and I wanted to focus my interest on the semiconductor area. In the first semester, I completed the Semiconductor Device Fabrication course, where Andy Grove's book was used as the textbook, and we experimented with metallization and other processes required for the fabrication of Metal-Oxide-Semiconductor (MOS) devices. I talked to Assistant Prof. Robert Pierret, who offered that course. I picked up a topic for doing a Master's degree project and dissertation on a topic relating to MOS capacitors. It involved the numerical calculation of low-frequency capacitance/voltage curves of MOS capacitors with nonconstant doping profiles by solving Poisson's Equations with the help of a fourth-order Runge-Kutta method. The master's thesis was mostly finished during the summer of 1969, and I submitted the written thesis in 1970 and was awarded the Master of Science (MS) in Electrical Engineering then. I published a paper in Electronics Letters, an international publication, on the results of my analysis of the CV Characteristics of MOS devices.

Doctoral Program

In the fall and spring semesters of the academic sessions 1969-1970, I enrolled in four graduate courses each semester, so that I completed all the doctoral course requirements. I also worked at Solid State Electronics Laboratory as a member of the laboratory to observe all the fabrication processes and research projects being pursued there. But Professor Robert Pierret left the University of Illinois to join Purdue University, and I had differences with Prof. C.T. Sah, the Head of the Solid-State Electronics Laboratory. So, at the beginning of the academic session 1970-1971, I moved to the Digital Computer Laboratory to pursue a doctoral thesis program there. I had already finished my course requirements for the PhD degree by taking many courses in solid state physics and quantum mechanics at the graduate level, in addition to my courses in electrical engineering and computer engineering. I audited a few graduate courses in artificial intelligence and machine learning to expose myself further to the new frontiers. I also performed an individual study on color information processing with one of the professors in the department of computer science.

During the academic year 1970-1971, I was a teaching assistant for the fall semester, helping Prof S.W. Lee of the Electromagnetics Laboratory, and did the grading of the graduate class assignments of the Electromagnetics course. For the spring semester, I helped with the grading of the class assignments in the Electronics Circuits course. In the meantime, I had chosen a doctoral project in the Digital Computer Laboratory, which involved building a special digital display system.

The doctoral project was based on Dr. Edwin Land's two-color perception theory, which said that only two colors, white and red, can produce a gamut of all colors. This was shown to be the case with the projection of a picture obtained through the superimposition of the red frames and the white frames of the scene taken by using white and red filters of a flywheel. A display system proved the same by using a two-layer phosphor 'Penetron' cathode ray tube driven by a black and white camera fitted with a piezo-electric ceramic filter for passing the red and white color versions of the scene. Color information processing in humans and computer systems was also investigated. The overall system was built over a period of two years by designing and fabricating all the printed circuit boards, and integrating the camera systems, special CRT, and the piezo-electric filter. The overall scenes capture and display system was demonstrated to the panel of professors as part of the final defense, along with the written thesis.

5. On the Road to Marriage

Early Marriage Proposal

After the summer of 1962 and during my pre-university college days at Rajendra College, proposals started coming for my early marriage. It became more of a reality after my cousins, Prafulla and Bamdev, were married in the spring of 1963. Their brides were still very young, and the actual consummation of marriage would happen in a few years when the bride reached puberty and the set of two families agreed on the dates. There was a serious proposal brought up by my brother-in-law, Judhistir Panda, for the daughter of a rich and powerful Brahmin farmer in his village of Chiladi. The proposed candidate was barely ten years old and had completed her education in the village primary school. I was completely opposed to this proposal and the tradition of child marriage prevalent in many villages of Ganjam. None of my friends or classmates in Balangir were in this state. No one would talk about marriage until one was all set up in a career track or was financially self-sufficient to start a family.

There was a stream of people coming from Bodoboranga to convince me to agree to this proposal. During one such visit, my cousin, who was the headmaster of the village school where I studied, came to Balangir to convince me. I always had a deep respect for his just conduct and behavior. Though I was never pressed by my eldest brother, it was assumed that I should go along with the proposal brought up by our brother-in-law. They started speaking about the honor of the family and other consequences if I did not agree to the proposed date of marriage to be held after our college examinations were completed. After the examinations for the theory papers were completed, I ran away from home with my friend Ganga Rath to his village near Balangir town for a few days. We had to come back to take the practical examination that was scheduled. The pressure was still on me, and I was not even eighteen years old yet.

Finally, I thought that I should not get married kicking and screaming since marriage comes only once in life! If I had to have this proposed marriage ceremony for the sake of family honor and my future, I must agree amicably and arrange things appropriately. So, I finally agreed to the marriage ceremony to be held in April 1963 in the village. The arrangements would happen in our village and the bride's village, which was a couple of km away.

The plan was for me to go and appear for the IIT Entrance examinations at Hirakud, Sambalpur, and then proceed directly to the village for the marriage ceremony. My brother-in-law accompanied me to Hirakud to ensure that I did not run away. So, after taking the examination at Hirakud, I left for Berhampur by bus along with my brother-in-law. From Berhampur, we went by bus to my brother-in-law's village and then walked up to his house. When we reached his house, we learned that the bride's father had canceled the marriage ceremony since he sensed my opposition to the proposal and wanted to protect the future of his daughter. I was happy that it had turned out that way. My eldest brother also reached our brother-in-law's house the following day and came to know about the same. So, we walked back to our village, just a couple of miles away, without ever talking to the bride's father. Thus ended my first encounter with the business of marriage!

I came back to the house in my village. My mother and brothers now fully accepted the fact that the marriage would not take place. A classmate of mine came from Balangir to attend the marriage since I had let them know that I was going to get married on the approved date. So, the marriage did not happen as planned, and after two weeks of staying in the village, I traveled by train to go back to Balangir through Vizianagaram in Andhra Pradesh. I decided then to visit Simhanchalam, which was only about thirty miles away from Vizianagaram, and offer my hair as thanks to the god Simhanchala at the top of the mountain there. I had never wished any form of support from God against this marriage. But, when I got free from this entangle, I just felt relieved and thankful that this had happened due to perhaps the unknown hands of the Almighty! This is perhaps the first time in my life that I went to the temple to thank God for what he had done!

As I had related in the last chapter, I was called for an interview at IIT, Kharagpur, after a couple of weeks. I went for the interview with hardly much hair on my head. Nobody asked me the reason for the shaved head during the interview or the mild ragging in the corridors of Azad Hall of Residence, where I stayed during the interview. Neither did I tell anyone about this odd marriage affair to any friend in engineering school. The fact that this marriage proposal from the family was finally canceled because of external forces, there was no more pressure on me to marry. I was free now to decide my course in life!

A Long Engagement

There was an unusual set of coincidences when I got back to my village after learning of the cancellation of the marriage ceremony. Our front-door neighbor was a good friend of my cousin, the headmaster of the village. She was mostly always living with her brother and mother in distant Kolkata, and my cousin would look after her house. But, during the last couple of years, she had come back to the village to stay, along with her mother. It so happened that her brother's family from Kolkata had just come to the village to spend part of their summer vacation. There was Gautam, who was a couple of years younger than me and was studying in a convent school in Ahmednagar, Maharashtra. He was under the supervision of his uncle, who was a heart surgeon at the Wanless Wadi Hospital nearby. His two sisters were Anuradha, about ten years old, and Sushma, about seven years old. Both of them were studying in school in South Kolkata. Gautam and I became good friends. For the two weeks that I was in the village, we would go every evening to the deep riverside to talk and relax. I told him about the books and the stories I had read from the translated literature. His younger sister, Sushma, would play with me and come to our house. His other sister, Anuradha, was more reticent and hardly talked to me. At the end of my vacation in the village, I parted from Gautam, and we decided to keep in touch with each other. At that time, I did not know that this encounter with Gautam, his mother, and the sisters would lead to a future trail of events a couple of years later around Kolkata!

I spent the summer of 1967 taking industrial training at Bharat Electronics Ltd (BEL) in Bengaluru. At the end of the training, I traveled to Kharagpur while stopping on the way to visit my village for a couple of days. I met my mother and my brother's family. I was very sad to learn that my cousin, the headmaster of the village school, had passed away a few months back due to a sudden deterioration of his health. I visited Gautam's aunt in the village before leaving. At that time, she just mentioned that her elder brother's daughter, Anuradha, was studying and doing quite well in the school in south Kolkata, and if the stars properly align, she could be a marriage partner with me. I did not say anything at the time. I just said that I planned to go abroad to the United States for further study after completing my degree at IIT Kharagpur next year.

I came back to IIT Kharagpur, and our final year of classes started. After a few days, I got a telegram from Gautam's uncle that he would be visiting Kolkata soon before his departure to Canada with his family. He asked me to meet him at his elder brother's flat in Kolkata.

Gautam's uncle had gone to Canada in 1952 for further medical studies after his MBBS training at SCB Medical College at Cuttack, Odisha. He had completed his FRCS at the University of Saskatchewan, worked in Canada for some time, and then returned to India with his family to serve the people. He had married a Canadian citizen and had a daughter and two sons. He had finally found a position at the Wanless Wadi Chest Hospital in Maharashtra and was well known to have performed the first open heart surgery in India. He was going back to Canada with his family after serving in India for six years, because he could not afford to arrange proper education for his three children and other reasons. Since I knew about him and he was also the best friend of my cousin, the headmaster who had just passed away, I wanted to meet him to get some pointers about going abroad for education.

I took a train from Kharagpur to Howrah the next Sunday afternoon. From Howrah station, I took a bus going to South Kolkata and got down at the crossing of Gariahat Road and Rash Behari Avenue. I searched for the address of the flat that was given in the telegram, but had much difficulty locating it because the entrance was quite inside and not very apparent from the side pavement. I went up the stairs and rang the bell. Gautam's uncle opened the door, and after a brief introduction, I sat down to talk with him at the table. This was late afternoon, and he told me that he was flying back to Canada to restart his medical career there. I told him the fact that I would be going to the United States of America or Canada for higher studies in the next year. It may take four to five years to complete the Master's and Ph.D. degrees there. At this time, a young girl came out of the bedroom, walked across, and went to the kitchen area. I recognized that she was Gautam's sister, Anuradha. I saw her after four years. She had now fully developed into a young lady. After having tea there, Dr. Padhi and I went down to have some snacks at the Quality Ice Cream restaurant on Gariahat Road. He told me there that his elder niece would be a good match for me when I was ready for marriage. He wanted to fix this proposal before he left for Canada. I told him to write to my eldest brother. He knew him while studying in the school in Chikiti Middle School.

He said that his elder brother was instrumental in providing him a medical education and sending him abroad for higher education, and that his brother was a very strict person who adhered to his duty at the office and the home. He told me that Gautam would be back in Kolkata to study after the completion of the present academic year.

In the evening, I did some shopping downstairs at the market along with Gautam's mother and sisters. After that, I took a stroll to the Birla Arts Center on Lake Avenue along with Anuradha and one of her friends from the adjoining flat. I had a chance to talk to Anuradha in more detail about what she was studying and what her interests were. She was interested in painting and was taking lessons at home from an Art teacher. She liked cooking and helping her mother, although they had a cook provided through the Railways Head office, where her father worked.

We looked at the displayed paintings in the galleries at Birla Center and then walked back on Lake Avenue to Rash Behari Avenue. At their flat, I also had a brief conversation with her father, Bhagirathi Padhi, who at the time was a very high-ranking official in the Railways Headquarters office. After having an early dinner at their flat, I left for Howrah to take the train to Kharagpur.

This trip to South Kolkata to meet Gautam's family and especially meet his sister Anuradha certainly evoked good vibrations within me for a possible future tie-up. Although they were brought up in a metropolitan environment, they had similar roots. Anuradha had her first few years of school at one of the American Schools in Kolkata. She was studying now at Southpoint High School. She was only fourteen years old then, and I was eight years older than her. In any case, I was not looking for any marriage in the next four to five years. So, I did not have any objection to the proposal for a future tie-up.

During my final year at IIT Kharagpur, I stopped at least two more times at Anuradha's house when I went to Kolkata to appear for the Graduate Records Examination (GRE) and later. After the final year examinations were over, I went back to Balangir with all my things from the hostel. I accepted the fellowship awarded by the University of Illinois to pursue the Master's and Ph.D. degrees in Electrical Engineering. However, I did not receive the required I-20 papers from the university to arrange for my trip to the United States. I stopped by Kharagpur and went to the Azad Hall of Residence to check if there was any mail for me. Indeed, there was mail from the University of Illinois, and they wanted me to send the results of the 'Test of English as a Foreign Language' (TOEFL) test. Since I had not taken the TOEFL test, I decided to take the Michigan Test. For that purpose, I went to Kolkata and stayed with Anuradha's family. My friend Gautam had already come back to Kolkata to study there. I stayed a few days and had a good time visiting different places around the city. As I interacted more with Anuradha, my attraction towards her increased, and we developed a quiet liking between us.

I came back during the month of August to Kolkata to make my final travel arrangements and attend the orientation seminar held at the American consulate for students going to the United States that year. Before that, I had convinced my mother and brother that I wanted to have an engagement with Anuradha before I left for the United States. That way, I would be sure to come back to India for a definite marriage ceremony after four to five years. Personally speaking, I was convinced that was the right thing to do since I didn't know how a person could come back to India in search of a bride, and then choose one in a couple of weeks, and then marry. Here, I had a future partner who was compatible with our two families, and I had already developed a romantic relationship with her.

As planned, I came to Kolkata the day before my flight. My second brother, Padmanna, and my nephew, Bhagavan, had come to bid me farewell. My brother had brought the gold ornaments to be given to Anuradha. So, the next day, we had a formal small engagement ceremony at Anuradha's house. At noon, we two went off to Victoria Memorial Garden to enjoy the environment there and talk in private. I flew that evening on 5th September with my friend Omprakash from Balangir, who was going to the University of Iowa for graduate studies in Electrical Engineering. Anuradha and her mother were at the airport to see me off.

Marriage

Anuradha and I corresponded with each other by letters every couple of months. That was not the age of phones and mobiles, and rapid communication. I never phoned her house in Kolkata, and neither did she. It was perhaps good, that old way, since both of us waited to get a letter and then reply to it over a period. Time passed by quickly that way. I used to write to her father, now and then, reporting to him the progress I was making at the University of Illinois. I was also in communication with her uncle's family in Regina, Saskatchewan province of Canada, and visited them in the summer of 1970 for a week or so.

A couple of weeks after I got back to the campus from Regina, I got a call from Anuradha's aunt, Emma Padhi in Regina, to convey to me the sad news of Gautam's death in Kolkata. It was a devastating blow to the whole family. Gautam was such a nice and handsome young man in his early twenties, studying for a Bachelor's degree in Commerce and working as an apprentice with a company. I had established an excellent rapport with him during my visits to their apartment in Kolkata before leaving for the United States. He had also written to me recently to send him a few things from the US that he needed.

It took some time for Anuradha's family to slowly recover from this tragedy. Her father established a temple trust in his ancestral village of Khajuria, a couple of km from Bodoboranga on the other side of the river Bahuda. A Radhakrishna temple was built along with some contributions and full participation by the village community. The temple has a large compound with many rooms for servitors and guests, and has a garden full of coconuts and other trees. It has cultivated land and suitable bank deposits for the maintenance of the temple. The board, consisting of the villagers with Anuradha's father as the chairman, performed the construction and management of the temple.

I wanted to go to India sometime in 1972 or 1973 before completing my doctoral thesis. The Kolkata area was going through a huge crisis before and during the 1971 December war with Pakistan, when Bangladesh was created, and the refugees were sent back to the newly created country. In the meantime, I got very bad news from my family that my eldest nephew, Bhagaban, my eldest brother's son, was diagnosed with blood cancer. He was taken to a hospital in Visakhapatnam for treatment, and the whole of my eldest brother's family was camping there. Bhagaban was four years younger than me, and we used to go to high school together in one cycle paddled by me, and did most other activities together in our locality. He was like a younger brother to me. He was studying for his Master's degree in commerce in Sambalpur when this happened. I wanted to visit India and see him.

In March 1972, I got the news of my nephew Bhagaban's death sometime after the amputation of his leg, where cancer had started. I was very sad at this turn of events and wanted to visit India. Anuradha's father wrote around this time that a marriage ceremony could be held in June 1972 if I came to India. Anuradha would have finished her higher secondary education then and come to the United States, and possibly pursue further studies.

I had already passed the preliminary examination

relating to the doctoral thesis proposal and talked with my advisors, Professor Bill Kubitz and Professor Ted Poppelbaum of Digital Computer Laboratory, and planned for a four-week vacation in India. A June 1st marriage date was decided. I made arrangements to get a married student's apartment and terminate my tenancy at Daniels Hall. I flew to Kolkata in the third week of May.

I stopped by for a day in Kolkata and then went to Berhampur. My second brother, Padmanna, had changed his base to Berhampur from Balangir and was engaged in the transport business from there. I went to the village and saw my mother and my third brother's family. We decided to have a low-key marriage ceremony in Kolkata only, keeping in view the tragic events three months back.

As planned, we went by train and stayed in rooms rented for the occasion in the same building at the junction of Gariahat Road and Rash Behari Avenue. The marriage ceremonies and feasts were held in a marriage mandap nearby in Ballygunge. My mother and family members from the village and Berhampur were present, in addition to a few of my friends, Surendra Purohit and Nalini Mohanty from Balangir. Upendra Kachru, who was with me at the University of Illinois and earlier at NIT – Rourkela, had come back to India and was working in Kolkata. He too attended the function. All of Anuradha's friends and their family friends, including some from Odisha, were present. Her uncle and aunt from Canada had come to attend the marriage. There was no dowry payment in the marriage ceremony, just a token payment of Rupees ten. There was also no feast or other paraphernalia from the groom's side in Kolkata or elsewhere.

We stayed in Kolkata for two days after the marriage and then came by train to Berhampur and stayed there for a day, and then went to our village and stayed for a couple of days with my mother in our ancestral house. From the village, we went by train to Balangir via Vizianagaram. We stayed with my eldest brother's family and also met all my friends there. We traveled back to Kolkata by train to arrange for the trip back to the United States. The registration of marriage was done in Kolkata, and a Visa was obtained for Anuradha as a dependent student wife. On the way to the United States, we stayed in Mumbai for two days and met M. Ramamurthy and Satyapriya Majumdar.

We flew to Chicago O'Hare airport and then took Ozark Airlines to fly to Champaign airport. My friend Sanak Mishra met with us at the airport and then drove us to Goodwin Apartments on Green Avenue in Urbana. A studio apartment was ready for us there.

Life started smoothly at Goodwin since it was a furnished apartment with all the necessary gizmos. My car was in the parking lot for shopping trips as needed. There were a few Indian families in the building, and Anuradha had become friends with a few of the ladies. I mostly focused on work and tried to complete my doctoral project within a year, but we participated in all suitable activities. Anuradha enrolled in a course to learn swimming. We went to Shelby Lake over the weekend for boat rides with friends. We went to Chicago to attend a conference organized by the American Hindu Association and visited the Vivekananda Ramakrishna Center at the University of Chicago.

In the fall of 1972, Anuradha enrolled in an Economics course at Parkland College in Champaign to get a taste of the American education system, but did not like it much and stopped attending it after a few weeks. During the Christmas break, we went along with Don Parsons in his car and visited his parents in the suburb of Toronto. We stayed there for a couple of days and toured the Toronto area, including Niagara Falls, and then came back to Urbana by bus.

In the spring of 1973, Anuradha learned typing, shorthand, and other skills by attending classes in Champaign. This came quite handy while typing my thesis and papers. I was close to getting ready to complete the doctoral project and started looking for a job in the industry. I had been called for interviews at Texas Instruments in Dallas and Burroughs Corporation in New Jersey. Once I got a job offer as a Senior Engineer at Burroughs, I scheduled my final defense of the thesis. I sailed through the final without much difficulty. I decided to join Burroughs in New Jersey later in June. I bought a new car, the Chrysler Dodge Dart model in a metallic green color, and gave away my old car to our friend Dhingra. I was now ready to drive through the plains and come to New Jersey.

We drove eastward through Illinois, Indiana, and then Ohio. As we were driving through Ohio, I pressed on the gas pedal during a flat stretch to test how fast the new car could go, and was immediately picked up by the highway patrolling police and given a speeding ticket. That was my only ticket for pressing on the gas pedal for a very long time.

We stopped on the way near Pittsburgh, Pennsylvania, to spend a night with the family of Prafulla Panigrahi. Prafulla joined the University of Illinois, Urbana-Champaign, to do his graduate studies in metallurgical engineering in September 1968. He had joined a local company in the Pittsburgh area after completing his master's degree around 1971. Prafulla's wife, Saila, was a very hospitable person and told us how they had taken care of accident victims of Indian descent from New Jersey traveling to the Pittsburgh area during a job search. I later met some of these grateful souls, talking highly of Saila in New Jersey.

Part II
The Work Years in America
(1973 to 1997)

06. Life in America
07. World of Semiconductors
08. World of Computers
09. World of Data Networks
10. World of Artificial Intelligence
11. Move from America to India

6. Life in America

Living in Piscataway, NJ

My life in New Jersey started when I arrived at the Holiday Inn at Piscataway on Highway 287 South in late June 1973 to stay there for two weeks before getting an apartment for rent in the area. I joined Burroughs Corporation at their Electronic Memory Systems Operation (EMSO) on Randolphville Road in Piscataway. We were able to sign a one-year lease agreement for the one-bedroom apartment nearby in Piscataway at Royal Gardens Apartments. It was just a few miles away from the office via the town roads or the highway.

We moved to Royal Gardens after a week and started furnishing it. We had to get a bed, a sofa, a dinette table, and a set of chairs for the kitchen. We were able to procure them fast from furniture stores in central Jersey. Our upstairs neighbor, an old German lady, was going back to Germany along with her husband for retirement and offered us to give away her special translucent large curtains and palmette for the large window in the drawing room. That made things easier for Anuradha to decorate the drawing room. We became friends with the German couple and their two daughters, who were living nearby. Her elder daughter invited us for dinner and discussions after a few weeks at her apartment on Route 22.

I found that two colleagues in my department at Burroughs, Farouk Quadri and Singh Yallamanchilli, also lived in the same apartment complex, just a few apartments away. There were also other Indian families next to our apartment: Sharma from Delhi, Kutte from Karnataka, Guru Singh from Ballia in Uttar Pradesh, and Malhotra from Punjab. There was a smorgasbord of India right next to us. All of the ladies were staying at home and taking care of their kids and family, and not working outside. Anuradha had a gala time in the daytime with these ladies partying and gossiping. Time passed very fast that summer and fall of 1973. In between, we went to Springfield, Massachusetts, in September to attend the marriage ceremony between our friends at the University of Illinois, Sanak Mishra, and Veena Paralkar. We had also earlier taken them and Veena's parents from India to visit Niagara Falls in New York State. Sanak and Veena returned to India later that year, and Sanak started working at Ranchi.

Anuradha accompanied me to Colorado and California when I went there for company work. In California, we stayed in San Diego and Escondido while I was interacting with Burroughs Micro Components Operation at San Bernado. We also went to Los Angeles and Las Vegas during the weekends to visit the various tourist attractions.

After all these travel and amusement activities, Anuradha realized that she had to now restart her education and study at a nearby college. After looking at the various possibilities, she enrolled at Middlesex College for a degree in accounting. She enrolled as a full-time student, and hence, we were very busy now, even during the weekends.

We stayed active and participated in most social and cultural activities going on in the New Jersey and New York areas. We participated in the activities of the Indian ethnic organizations. I was appointed as Vice-President of the Association of Indians in America (AIA). At the time, Professor Manoranjan Dutta of the Department of Economics at Rutgers University was the President of AIA. Anuradha and I attended many of the dinner meetings of the AIA management and before and during major functions. I especially remember sponsoring a musical night with the famous Sitar player Ali Akbar Khan in New Jersey. AIA also helped the Indian refugees who came from North Africa, where they were displaced from Uganda and other countries.

In the summer of 1974, we took a long tour by car to Moose Jaw, Saskatchewan province of Canada, to meet Anuradha's uncle's family. We drove from New Jersey to Chicago and stayed there the night, and then drove to North Dakota and halted there for one night. The next day, we reached Moose Jaw in the evening. Dr. Padhi was serving as a surgeon at the local hospital. His children, Pamela, Desmond, and Dev Kumar, were studying in the school. We spent plenty of time at their house in Moose Jaw and the cottage at the nearby lake, where there was boating and plenty of gardening. After a week of relaxation there with the family, we left for Calgary in Alberta province.

We stayed in Calgary for a day, and after looking around the city attractions, we left for Banff to see Lake Louise. Banff was only about eighty miles from Calgary and took us about two hours. The scene at Lake Louise was serene and beautiful. After enjoying it for hours, we left Banff on our way to Yellowstone National Park in the United States. It was a long and lonely drive, and we stayed in the park for two days and saw the 'Old Faithful' hot spring and the lakes around the park. From here, we drove to Ames, Iowa, and stayed a day with Omprakash. From there, it was a long drive back to New Jersey, and we made it in two days while staying nights on the way. We got back to Piscataway just around the Labor Day holiday.

Anuradha was back in college and busy for the whole of the academic year 1974 to 1975 at Middlesex College. She finished all the course requirements for the associate degree in the summer of 1975 and started working as an Assistant Accountant at Sterling Extruder, a small manufacturing company in Piscataway. She also enrolled in the evening classes for a Bachelor's program in Accounting at Rutgers University, New Brunswick. So, she was doubly busy now.

Around this time, we met a family from Odisha who were staying in New Brunswick: Ram Saran and Prabasini Sahu and their three children. Through them, we met Dibakar and Prabha Panigrahi of South Brunswick and got introduced to the Odisha Society of America (OSA). We attended all of the cultural functions organized by OSA in the tri-state area and got to meet many families from Odisha residing in the eastern United States. The NY-NJ chapter of OSA regularly held cultural functions in the tri-state area.

At this time, we looked around for a new residence and decided to buy a new house that was being completed in East Windsor, a town further south in Mercer County. It was centrally located and connected through highways and not very far from Piscataway or New Brunswick. So, we moved to our new house at 5 Cedar Lane in East Windsor in December 1975.

Living in East Windsor, NJ

The house on 5 Cedar Lane in East Windsor, New Jersey, was a three-bedroom colonial house with three bedrooms on the top floor. The house was a new one, and hence, we had to take care of the new lawn in the front and back in the spring season after a couple of months. The immediate problem in the house was getting used to the forced hot air heating system that was fired by the gas furnace. The air was too dry inside in December when we moved. I had to put together a water sprinkling system to send some moisture along with the hot air. In the spring, when it rained a lot, the motor connected to the sump pump in the basement ran continuously to pump out water. Our lawn came out fine after the seeding. We planted flower trees, dogwood, Exira, etc., and a few fruit trees, pears, and apples. In summer, we had a small vegetable garden at the very back. Behind our property were fields where corn was being harvested. We planted a row of tall poplar trees at the back.

I was busy during the weekend with yard work, but on other days commuted by car to work at the Piscataway plant of Burroughs. I applied for jobs at Bell Laboratories around this time and decided to join their Holmdel location in the Network Systems group. Before joining, Anuradha and I took a trip to India to visit our families. We visited Kolkata, Cuttack, Berhampur, and our village, and then, to Balangir to see my mother and my eldest brother's family. We returned to Kolkata by train, and I flew back to New York, but Anuradha stayed a couple of more weeks with her parents.

Anuradha finally came back since she had enrolled in a few evening courses at Rutgers University as part of her Bachelor's program in accounting. She also secured a job with a small chemical company in East Windsor. That was very convenient for her to work and just take a long commute for the classes in the evening. It was not a long commute for me to Holmdel Bell Laboratories, about the same time, but a shorter distance compared to commuting to Piscataway. Later on, I joined a carpool of people working at Holmdel Bell Lab. So, the change of work to Bell Labs was relatively smooth from these perspectives.

We got to know a few Indian families in this new development: Makhijani, Deshpande, and an Indian family from the East Indies. We also met a few families from Odisha in the nearby towns: Sadananda Barik from the 1968 batch of NIT-Rourkela and others. We continued our activities with AIA and also joined the Indian cultural activities around the New Brunswick campus of Rutgers University.

Through the work environment at Bell Laboratories, we became friends with many Indian and American families. Anuradha changed her job and worked at Trenton for the New Jersey Government for a year in their finance department, and it was not a long commute to work for her. After she completed her Bachelor of Science in Accounting with High Honors from Rutgers University, she applied and secured a job at Holmdel Bell Laboratories as a financial assistant. So, now we drove to work together in one car to Holmdel. She worked in the planning and budgeting department and interfaced with all the departments in the Bell Laboratories.

Now that we were settled in our jobs and Anuradha had completed her degree, we started thinking about starting a family. We had disappointments when an ovarian pregnancy was detected. Fortunately, Dr. Franzoni, her gynecologist at Trenton, removed that successfully through laparoscopic surgery.

I had by now worked at Bell Laboratories for three years in the systems department, first in defining product requirements and then performing project analysis, and did not like the prospects of the project. I wanted to make a change without moving out and disrupting Anuradha's work. I secured a job at RCA Solid State Division in Somerville. NJ. It was not a long commute north from East Windsor, and I joined work there in September 1979. At this time, we looked for a new house around the Somerville area and found a new large development being started in Branchburg, the town south of Somerville. We booked the construction of this new house in October 1979 and moved there in April 1980 when it was ready.

Living in Branchburg, NJ

The house at 15 Arrowhead Drive, Branchburg, was a four-bedroom and spacious colonial house on an acre lot. It was a lot of 150 feet wide and more than 300 feet in depth, all grass except for a half dozen large trees on the left side. The front lawn was prepared with sod grass blocks, and the back portion with seeds planted. There was plenty of work for me doing the brick patio at the back, right behind the kitchen and dinette. A large bay window provided a magnificent view of the rolling grass meadows behind. The physical move from East Windsor to Branchburg was very smooth since the movers packed it up in the morning, moved everything on the truck, and placed the things in the new house that afternoon.

Anuradha was busy decorating the rooms with specially designed drapes for the windows. I planted rhododendron, Exira, and other flower shrubs in the front of the house. The change to the new and beautifully situated house on a hill was a very pleasant one. Anuradha commuted to her job at Holmdel in a carpool. For me, it was just a five-minute ride down the state highway. One of my colleagues from Bell Laboratories, Pramod Verma, also moved to the same residential development, and we established rapport with the neighbors.

After being in the Branchburg house for a couple of months, Anuradha thought she was pregnant. We confirmed that after a visit with Dr. Franzoni in Trenton. Our life was now carefully planned not to take any unnecessary long drives and to avoid heavy work on her part. After a few months, we went through future parent orientation to learn about the processes relating to childbirth and care. Anuradha's mother could not come since her sister was to be married around that time. However, her aunt from Canada would come around the time of delivery to help us. Since she was a trained nurse, it would be beneficial in the American environment.

There were no complications during the whole pregnancy period. Anuradha took a leave of absence from Bell Laboratories once she was seven months pregnant and planned to rejoin work a few months after the birth of the child. Anuradha's aunt Emma Padhi flew down from Regina, Canada, and arrived. The following day, the temperature was in the low sixties and very warm for a winter day. Anuradha started feeling the upcoming arrival. So, I drove her along with her aunt to Trenton and admitted her into the hospital as per the advice of the doctor. Aunt and I came back home to rest that night. We went back the next morning to the hospital. It was a very special day on 20th January 1981. Ronald Reagan took the oath as the President of the United States in the morning in Washington. The hostages held by the government of Iran were finally released on that day. Anuradha gave birth to a boy that evening at St. Francis Hospital in Trenton. We named him Arun Ranjan Panigrahi. I held him and put him in a bed for the newborn. There was a small smile on the baby's face,

I thought. I came back home along with our aunt Emma Padhi to the house in Branchburg. I took two days off from work to prepare things at home and bring both mother and child home. We were all happy that everything turned out well. Anuradha's aunt left for Canada after a few days.

We already had a room wallpapered to be the baby's room next to the master bedroom. The nurses had given the baby milk bottles during the hospital stay, and he was not sucking enough to get milk from the mother. We did not realize this until about two weeks, while he was getting weaker. We saw a new pediatrician right in our locality and immediately supplemented his food and drinks, and he recovered. This was our first big lesson as new parents. Anuradha took care of the baby with some more tips from our friend, Prabasini Sahu, who lived in nearby New Brunswick.

There were some changes in the organizational structure at RCA around this time, and it was apparent to me that RCA was in the process of unloading some of these businesses. So, I started looking for a job elsewhere. I remember flying to the Minneapolis area along with Arun when he was barely four months old. In the summer of 1981, I interviewed with the semiconductor division of Digital Equipment Corporation in the suburb of Boston and joined there as an Engineering Manager in September 1981. It meant all of us moving to the Boston area. I had already convinced Anuradha that there was no point in her going back to the job waiting at Bell Laboratories, and she should take a couple of years off to take care of the child and pursue her goal of an MBA degree. We looked for housing in the towns around Marlborough, where I was to start work, and it was very difficult to buy an old house that fitted all our requirements. We selected a new house to be built on the side of a small hill in Westborough, right next to Route 9. We had to wait until June 1982 to take possession of the house. So, for eight months, I commuted to Marlborough every week on Monday morning and then stayed at a rented apartment during the week.

Living in Westborough, MA

The new house at Westborough was finally completed to our specifications towards the end of May 1982. It was a four-bedroom colonial-style house with four bedrooms on the top floor. There was an open balcony next to the master bedroom, which we converted after a couple of years into a jacuzzi room with glass windows on all three sides. On the ground floor, we had a large drawing room, dining room, kitchen, and a covered balcony next to the drawing room, which was later closed with all floor-length glass panes and a window to provide a serene view of the woods and act as a sun room in winter. But the other real specialty of this house was the large 22 feet by 22 feet area over the double garage that I designed into a long ten feet wide study room for myself and my son, and the rest into a family room with a fireplace. The basement underneath the house opened to the double garage and was later finished to allow us to have large social gatherings where people can walk straight into the basement.

We finally moved to the house at 19 Nottingham Lane, Westborough, along with our furniture and other belongings, and got settled. It was now for Anuradha to get the house decorated with the drapes. We had already got the rooms wallpapered as part of the construction. There was a lot of work outside taking care of the new lawn and preparing the back terrain of the house that was rising at the back with hundreds of trees. I had to cut a few of the trees to make a sitting and gardening plateau on the hill. Adjacent to the wooden deck behind the house, I made a small decorative fountain.

It was difficult for Anuradha to stay at home as she was used to working outside, and she was now in a completely new environment as a young new mother. She struggled to keep herself busy decorating the house, making small artifacts and furniture pieces, and above all, taking care of Arun. She also enrolled in a part-time graduate MBA program in the evening at Framingham College, which was located not very far from our house.

In January 1983, the whole family visited India. We observed Arun's second birthday in Kolkata along with Anuradha's parents, sister, and friends. We visited Balangir to meet my mother, my eldest brother's family, and friends. My mother was delighted to see us and happy that her youngest child had a son. We met my classmates during a dinner at a restaurant there. I flew back from Kolkata after a vacation of about three weeks to join work. But Anuradha stayed back for a few more weeks and flew back along with her mother, Hemlata Padhi.

My mother-in-law enjoyed staying with us and taking care of baby Arun. It became easier for Anuradha to take care of things at home, and she signed up for more courses at Framingham College. She completed her Master's degree in 1984 and applied for a job at Digital Equipment Corporation. She joined DEC's Hudson LSI facility as a financial analyst. Arun started going to the nursery school, which was just one house away, and my mother-in-law took care of taking and bringing Arun. So, life was very smooth and relaxing. She stayed with us for about five years at Westborough, and it was an incredible amount of help to us and Arun. As Arun started going to

Westborough's Hastings primary school, she would also walk along with him to the school, one km away from our house, but passing through two major junctions in the town. She would also pick him up after school was over. There was a beautiful relationship between Arun and his grandmother that benefited him all his life, all because of the special attention that he got during the early years. He was never left with a babysitter during his childhood. He spoke in Odia with her and in English with us, and thus became bilingual from early childhood. He also saw and heard Hindi movies and songs, along with English programs. At this time, we started the Odisha Society of Massachusetts, and our house had become a center for the Odia school for children and cultural events. We had hosted artists from Odisha: singer and music director Prafulla Kar, dancer Sanjukta Panigrahi, and her husband, singer Raghunath Panigrahi. One of the last musical functions in our basement was when singers Pranab Patnaik and Bhuvaneswari Mishra sang for the members. When Sangeeta Mahapatra and her sister came in 1996, they sang for the group in our drawing room. We had developed a close relationship with many families during our stay there. Satyabrata and Dola Mishra and their two children, Lubu and Lira, were from the next town of Shrewsbury. Budhinath and Kalyani Padhi and their two children, Vijaya and Vivek, were from the town of Northborough. Nityanand and Nihar Mishra and their two children, Vinita and Sunita, were from the town of Hopkinton, just a few km south. Amaresh and Sadhna Mahapatra and their three children, Surabhi, Arnab, and Sohini, were from the town of Acton, further up north east. Bijoy and Subarna Mishra and their children, Rekha and Siddu, were from the town of Cambridge. Arun was privileged to have grown up with all of these children and their parents, and hopefully, the relationship endures the time and distance.

When Arun was six years old, I enrolled him to take piano lessons, and he kept that up for the next ten years. Steve James, his piano teacher, came to our house to teach him once a week. Steve became a good family friend, and we had many interesting dinner discussions with him. Arun also learnt violin at school and was part of the school chorus singing group.

Arun played soccer, football, and basketball in school, and I fixed a basketball pole for practice in the backyard. I did not help him to play baseball as most American fathers did, because I did not know or have any interest in baseball. However, I compensated by teaching and playing tennis with him from the early years. He became part of his high school tennis team that had advanced to the final in a statewide competition.

We stayed in Westborough in the house on Nottingham Road for more than fifteen years while I worked at different divisions of Digital Equipment Corporation and later Process Software Corporation, and Data General. Anuradha also worked at various locations of Digital Equipment Corporation while staying here. I had done extensive work on the house by finishing part of the basement, adding a jacuzzi room on the top floor, and an extra glassed sitting room on the first floor. It was very conveniently located close to the highways. The township of Westborough was a small one with only about fifteen thousand residents and good schools, and a good public library. We thoroughly enjoyed our stay there and never had any problem with neighbors or the people of the town. Arun had a strong bond with his school friends. So, it was difficult to say goodbye to the house and Westborough when the time came to do that in 1997.

7. World of Semiconductors

The semiconductors are the basic building blocks of all modern equipment and systems. Semiconductor chips are produced after going through a very sophisticated process of fabrication that employs several steps of deposition, etching, cleaning, etc., with the help of high-resolution manufacturing systems. The chips are then probed for their functionality, marked, and then cut into separate chips from the base of round semiconductor wafers of sizes three to five inches in diameter, during those days in the seventies.

I was well prepared to work in the field of semiconductors due to my exposure and training at the University of Illinois. I was exposed to device physics, fabrication techniques, and digital applications in computer systems. So, during my work years in America, I had several opportunities at various companies to work on semiconductors, and that is described in this chapter.

Burroughs Corporation (1973 to 1976)

In the spring of 1973, I had interviewed at Burroughs Corporation. There were many questions and discussions on the computer industry. Burroughs Corporation was the vendor that was awarded to build the large parallel processor computer systems of 256 central processing units (CPUs) being installed at the University of Illinois, Urbana campus. So, there were questions on this supercomputer, called the Iliac IV computer, and other trends in the industry in the supercomputer area, and the semiconductor technologies employed. The following week, I was offered the position of Senior Engineer in the Advanced Development group of the engineering organization at Burroughs Electronic Memory Systems Organization (EMSO). I accepted the offer from Burroughs Corporation and decided to join them immediately after the completion of the defense of doctoral thesis.

The domains of semiconductors and computers were intimately related to each other from the very early days. As computers increased their power and complexity, they needed more powerful and complex integrated circuits (ICs) in the 1970s and 1980s. Computer companies were driving the complexity of integrated circuits as one of the major applications of these devices. The large computer companies worked with the different semiconductor companies to procure the next generation of integrated circuits for their new generation of computers. The development of new integrated circuits was so integral to the development of new families of computers that the larger computer companies established their semiconductor divisions to develop specialized integrated circuits catering to their custom needs and depended upon the semiconductor companies for other general integrated circuits. Thus, most of the mainframe computer companies, such as IBM, Burroughs, Univac, etc., and large mini-computer companies, such as DEC, had established their semiconductor divisions.

At the time, Burroughs was the second biggest mainframe computer company behind IBM. One of the projects was to develop a plan to set up a semiconductor operation on the eastern coast of America, similar to the one Burroughs had at Rancho Benardo near San Diego. We made various plans for a semiconductor manufacturing plant, focusing on the fabrication of LSI memory devices employing the latest technology, using the semiconductor wafer size of five inches in diameter. One obvious application of such a plant would be to manufacture emergent charge-coupled devices (CCD) of high speed and capacity.

The charge-coupled device technology was developed at Bell Telephone Laboratories just recently. There was special interest in applying these devices to build a disk-like solid-state memory system that would be an order faster than the mechanical disk devices. I designed an experimental CCD shift register device to be manufactured at the Rancho Bernardo plant of Burroughs Corporation, and spent a month or more living in Escondido, a nearby town, for that purpose.

We also worked on various applications of change-coupled device configurations, for example, content-addressable special memory subsystems. At the device level, CCD serial registers were designed and fabricated at the semiconductor facilities in Rancho Benardo to assess the reliability of manufacturing these devices.

There was an interim period of a couple of years when CCD memory had possible applications in building fast electronic disks. But, subsequently, Random Access Memory (RAM) devices kept on increasing their density and size due to the volume and level of investment. Hence, CCD memory applications disappeared. However, applications of CCDs as cameras and signal processing devices have persisted to this day. Boyle and Smith of Bell Telephone Laboratories were awarded the Nobel Prize in Physics in 2009 for the development of CCD technology. The CCD concept started in 1969 at Bell Laboratories, but it took decades to be implemented as commercial devices. It was exciting to be part of that transition phase in the mid-seventies when CCD technology had a very high promise.

I was granted five patents in the area of CCD device application and system organization during my work at Burroughs Corporation.

After three years of work in the Advanced Development group at Burroughs, I left the company to join Bell Telephone Laboratories at Holmdel, New Jersey, to work in the data network systems area. That meant moving away for about three years from the world of semiconductors, but I would rejoin to work on semiconductors again in the year 1979. Of course, I had written a couple of invited articles during this intervening time on CCD technology, the memory devices, and the test techniques. People I worked with at Burroughs in the above efforts were Marvin Steiner, Kent McKune, Satish Rege, and others.

RCA Solid State Division (1979 to 1981)
My next direct involvement in the semiconductor world was when I joined the RCA Solid State Division. Looking for a change from the world of computer networking at the moment at Bell Laboratories, I joined for work at RCA Solid State Division (SSD) at Somerville, NJ. I joined as a leader of Technical Staff in the organization that provided the radiation-hardened CMOS microprocessor and peripheral devices, plus SSI/MSI devices for applications in space projects sponsored by the government of the United States of America. My group was entrusted with the responsibility for probing and testing the integrated circuit devices and also for exposing them to the right amount of radiation to harden them for space applications.

One of the main projects requiring radiation-hardened devices was the Mariner project of the Jet Propulsion Laboratory (JPL) at California Technology (Caltech) in Pasadena, and it was sponsored by NASA (National

Aeronautics and Space Administration) of the United States. The spaceship was planned for launch to Mars. I visited JPL a couple of times to coordinate with the project management personnel there. This was the only defense or space project that I would ever work for industry in the United States. It did not require secret clearance from the U.S. government to manage the project. However, I could not enter the radiation–hardening chamber, which was operated by the personnel under my management.

One specialty of the organization under my management was a small manufacturing operation where a couple of operators and a technician performed the probe and test of the finished wafers. This was a three-shift operation and part of the manufacturing operation. These personnel were the members of the labor union at the SSD plant. So, I had to interact with the Union management and especially remember the luncheon that I had arranged for all the members of the Union Management at the successful completion of one of the projects.

Another challenging project at RCA was the development of a Generalized Test Program Generator that was engineered along with the RCA Government Systems Division at Moorestown, NJ. It allowed the device test engineers and product engineers to modify the baseline test cells to a user-specified sequence, resulting in a new device test program. This was designed for the RCA CMOS logic circuits for generating the test programs on the Teradyne J283 test systems. Under me, I had test and product engineers responsible for the rad-hard CMOS devices. I had visited many times, the plant at Findley, Ohio, and the one at Palm Beach, Florida, to help in the product engineering related to the assembly, packaging, and testing of these devices.

The development of CMOS and memory circuits at

RCA was focused primarily on low-power applications, the space application being the one further emphasizing the high-reliability and the radiation-hardening aspects relating to systems development. RCA had kept its semiconductor activities limited to CMOS circuits only and hence had become a niche player in the semiconductor world. It was no wonder that this division was divested from RCA subsequently. The two years spent here were memorable for the events in my life. I had further hands-on and management experience that helped me in the next assignment in the area of product engineering of the semiconductor devices at Digital Equipment Corporation. The people I worked with at RCA were Gene Reiss, Ed Farina, Bob Sewell, and many others.

DEC LSI Division (1981 to 1987)

Since there was little scope for growth at RCA at the time, I left RCA and joined Digital Equipment Corporation (DEC) in their LSI Division at Marlborough, Massachusetts, in September 1981. I was looking for a change where I could settle down for ten or more years in an environment of growth. The opportunity at DEC offered that possibility in Massachusetts. It was especially attractive to move to work outside of the Boston area, where a large number of computer and electronics companies were located. This required a physical move of the family from New Jersey to Massachusetts, and I was prepared for it.

I moved to Massachusetts to join the semiconductor organization of Digital Equipment Corporation and took charge of product engineering of microprocessors, peripheral circuits, programmable logic, and memory devices. In this capacity, I had to interface with all the leading semiconductor companies worldwide regarding their latest plans for the next generation of devices and technologies. As the Manager for the microprocessor, peripheral, memory, and programmable logic devices, I had the responsibility for developing the test programs required and then performing the product engineering related to quality and reliability associated with these LSI devices. Later on, analog and SSI/MSI devices were also added to this responsibility. Four to five supervisors and technical leaders had the specific responsibility for one or more of these product lines.

We had to interface extensively with all the semiconductor companies manufacturing these devices regarding the complexity and organization of the marketed and planned devices and the associated product data on quality and reliability. For the microprocessor, microcontroller, and peripheral devices, we often visited Intel, AMD, National Semiconductor, and Motorola in the USA and Hitachi, Fujitsu, and NEC in Japan. For memory devices, the main vendors at the time were National Semi, Motorola, Intel, Fujitsu, etc. South Korean semiconductor memory companies, such as Samsung, were just starting at the time to get into the memory arena. In the peripheral device area, there were some specialized device manufacturers, such as Western Digital, etc., who were the main vendors, in addition to all the above American and Japanese semiconductor companies. In the programmable logic device (PLD) area, the dominant vendors were AMD and Altera.

In the linear device area, National Semi, Analog Devices, Linear Technology, etc., were the main vendors. A whole set of new vendors focusing on linear and mixed signal devices also started in the mid-1980s.

Interacting with the major semiconductor vendors from the USA, Japan, and Europe, and keeping abreast of the latest LSI development, was one of the main activities. I often traveled to California, Texas, and Arizona to visit the semiconductor companies. In 1986, I also took a two-week trip to Japan to visit Fujitsu, Hitachi, NEC, and others to talk about the latest 32-bit microprocessor and peripheral circuits that were in the pipeline in these companies. At the time, there was an Industrial Exhibition at Tsukuba Prefecture, and we visited that too. We stayed at the Hotel New Otani at the center of Tokyo and spent most of the evenings being guests at the dinners arranged by the host semiconductor companies. There was plenty of interaction at these dinners with the geisha girls since they were employed by the hosts to ensure that we ate and drank enough and played enough!

Interacting with the major LSI Test vendors regarding their latest system offerings and evaluating the performance of these systems against the requirements at DEC was an important responsibility. We evaluated test systems from Teradyne, Tektronix, etc., and visited them often to assess their capabilities.

To assess the quality and reliability of the LSI devices, we subjected sample devices to go through extensive burn-in and subsequent reliability and performance tests. This was a key step that all LSI devices were subjected to assess the long-term reliability of these devices.

To establish an economic and sustainable availability of LSI devices, annual negotiations were held with all semiconductor vendors regarding price and availability, and the engineering organization actively supported this effort.

Another challenging responsibility was the publication of a newsletter within the company to inform the users regarding the advent of the latest LSI devices, and I published a newsletter that got circulated in the company.

There were a couple of application engineers who consulted with the different customers within DEC to apprise them of the latest devices and also to consolidate any special requirements for feedback to the semiconductor companies. During this time, I was also one of the Editors of IEEE MICRO Computer Magazine and had the opportunity to review many articles to be published in that professional monthly publication. The people I worked with at the LSI group of DEC were Dan Hamel, Prakash Bhalerao, Mike Misiaszek, Bill McCarthy, Rekula Reddy, Rick Chumsae, Kevin Sembrat, and many others. Prakash was the one who had hired me, and later we became colleagues. Prakash moved to California later and started a few successful companies, becoming a billionaire! Hats off to him for his entrepreneurship!

In the fall of 1987, I transferred from the LSI division of DEC to the Disk Subsystems organization after a tenure of six years at the LSI group. I had decided at the time that there was no scope for any semiconductor industry in India, and hence it was futile for me to get more experience in that area anymore. I had prepared a project proposal for establishing a semiconductor Assembly and Test facility in Odisha, along with a classmate of mine from NIT, Rourkela. At the time, such facilities had been established in Singapore and Malaysia. However, further analysis convinced me that it was not possible to have any such facility in India without significant government assistance. There was no scope for any such subsidy from the Government of India at the time. I also realized that my partner was not that clear about relocating to India, and was looking for some other benefits by participating in the project.

As stated in this chapter, 1987 was the last time I worked directly in a semiconductor facility. The four years after that, I focused on disk subsystems development and high-end computer systems development. 1991 was the last time I worked directly in the hardware systems development groups, which entailed keeping track of the latest LSI development in the industry.

8. World of Computers

My experience in the Digital Computer Laboratory at the University of Illinois had prepared me well to work in the world of computers. I was exposed to different hardware engineering projects relating to video transformation processors, new display systems technology, prosthetics, and robotics. I was also exposed to the design and applications of the Iliac IV parallel computer, consisting of four clusters of sixty-four processors each, developed with support from the United States Government and manufactured by Burroughs Corporation. That was my first level of direct engagement in computing technology and systems. We had a shop to fabricate electronic circuit boards designed to our specifications for use in the digital systems. We were building them as part of research to prove the viability of computing applications. This design and manufacturing process was similar to what was current in the computer industry, and hence, there was added confidence to work in the computer industry.

Burroughs Corporation (1973 to 1976)

At the time, Burroughs Corporation was one of the five companies that were in the business of making mainframe computers, the other being IBM, Sperry, NCR, and Univac. Burroughs was next to IBM in the range of computer systems provided, and its momentum of financial profitability and market growth. As stated earlier in the last chapter, I had joined a position in Burroughs Corporation at their Electronic Memory Systems Operation (EMSO) at Piscataway in New Jersey. The Burroughs EMSO plant had been making the magnetic core memory systems for all the lines of Burroughs Mainframe computers. More recently, they have been designing and making memory systems using the 1K and 4K memory integrated circuits procured from semiconductor companies. The Advanced Development group was spearheading new projects in three areas: 1. Memory systems utilizing new IC memories of density 32k and higher, 2. Establishing a new IC facility to design and manufacture such latest memory devices as described in the last chapter, and 3. Magnetic memory systems with the latest developments in magnetic bubble memory devices.

One of the main projects at the Burroughs EMSO plant was to examine the work toward developing the high-speed and high-density storage systems for application in the range of computers offered by Burroughs. At that time, Burroughs offered four families of computer systems: Small Systems, Medium Systems, Large Systems, and Special Systems. The Special Systems groups in the Great Valley Laboratory in the suburb of Philadelphia were the ones who were pushing for the high-speed memory systems. This was understandable since they were the ones who had supplied the Iliac IV Parallel Computer and were now looking for the development of a commercial system based upon parallel processing that could be marketed on a limited basis. Of course, they were the old days when there were very few applications that were amenable to parallel processing. Weather processing and defense applications were a few such ones supported by the government. There were no gaming applications or AI applications requiring massive computing as it is today. Even in those limited and other applications, the overall performance was limited by the performance of the memory systems. Hence, there was a requirement for extremely fast memory systems that could act as very fast disk systems. Charge-Coupled Devices and Magnetic Bubble Systems provided some solutions in these applications.

At the time, the CCD technology was being driven by the research departments at Bell Laboratories, Murray Hill, New Jersey. The group consisting of W.S. Boyle, G.E. Smith, C.H. Sequin, M.F. Tompsett, G.F. Amelio, and others had developed the CCD technology in 1970, and one of the main applications was as fast serial memories that could replace or supplement disk subsystems in the mainframe computer.

There was intense research as to how the CCD memory devices could be used in all kinds of computer applications, such as content-addressable memory subsystems, and other such novel applications of this newly developed technology.

We interfaced widely with all the semiconductor vendors working in the area of CCD memories at the time. Intel and Fairchild Semiconductor were the earliest to announce CCD commercial memory devices: both 16 kbit and 32 kbit devices.

In the meantime, there was an intense push from the semiconductor companies to develop a commercial CCD memory chip of high diversity. Intel was the first company to announce the availability of a 32kbit CCD memory device. So, we designed a CCD memory subsystem of 1Mbit using thirty-two such devices in a printed circuit board along with the associated driving circuits. This was the experimental system that we played with to ascertain its performance and application with the different Burroughs computer systems.

One interesting anecdote in 1976 was when we visited Intel Corporation in Silicon Valley and Mike Markkula, the Intel Marketing Manager, who was hosting us, announced at the luncheon in the restaurant that he was leaving Intel to head a small start-up personal computers company. Later, I found that he was joining the company, Apple Computer, started by Steve Jobs, as the President. Markkula was at the helm of Apple for the first few years.

DEC Disk Subsystems (1987-1990)

I worked at the Disk Subsystem group at Marlborough and Shrewsbury in Massachusetts for about three years from 1987 to 1990 at Digital Equipment Corporation (DEC). As a Senior Engineering Manager, I managed groups that were entrusted with test generation and performance measurement of the disks and the subsystems. During this time, we developed 5Mbit, 10 Mbit, and higher capacity disk devices with a special digital serial interface and their controller circuits, bundled as a disk subsystem for use in the various DEC systems, especially the personal computers and low-end minicomputer systems. These disk devices had a different interface specification called DSSI (Digital Serial System Interface) as opposed to SCSI, which was the standard in the industry. DSSI disks were supposed to have better performance compared to SCSI disks.

The group was part of the Storage Systems Division. Disks with higher capacity and performance were being developed at that time at the Colorado Springs facility of DEC.

A key responsibility was to develop the test and verification of the functionality of these devices and sub-systems. Another activity was to execute the various performance tests under different conditions for the disk and controller products. We were first in a facility in Marlborough, Massachusetts. But later, we moved to the new facility in Shrewsbury, Massachusetts, when the new building for the Storage Division of DEC was built there.

Some of the people that I worked with here were Bob Passmore, Shyam Parekh, Fred Vasconcelos, Suresh Jasrasaria, and many others.

DEC High Performance Systems (1991)

I joined the High-Performance Systems development of DEC in 1990. Our focus at the time was to develop the most cost-effective version of DEC's largest computer systems. I worked as a senior product manager and looked at the competitive environment and the market requirements of such systems. One responsibility here was to look at the architecture of multi-processors based on the use of commercially available microprocessor devices to arrive at cost-effective systems of high performance. A few niche computer companies had come up at this time, offering such multiprocessing computers for specialized applications.

This was a short-term assignment within Digital Equipment Corporation at its large Marlborough facility, not very far from my house in Westborough. DEC was competing at the high end with mainframe computer companies, and was being squeezed at the low end by the personal computer systems. So, DEC was going through plenty of turmoil trying to decide on the long-term strategy and investments. Soon after, I joined the DEC PC Networking group in Littleton, Massachusetts, further north of Marlborough on Highway 485. I was back to working in the area of computer networking after a gap of about eleven years, when I worked on semiconductors and computer hardware systems.

Data General Corporation (1996)

I joined the Data General Systems group as the director of the software applications development group that designed the computer system interfaces in the Data General systems. Data General at the time was the second biggest minicomputer company next to Digital Equipment Corporation, and was primarily located in Westborough, along with its headquarters. I reported to the Vice President of Software Engineering, who was located at the Raley, North Carolina. All of the Data General system and application software development and support groups were located at Raley, except for my group at Westborough. So, I had to make many trips to Raley to attend some of the group meetings there.

I left Data General in the late summer of 1996 after being there for a few months and went on a trip along with Anuradha and Arun to enjoy a vacation in different countries of Europe, before my eventual move to India in 1997.

9. World of Data Networks

Data Networking is a very challenging area that examines the proper interconnection of computers and other data devices and the communication between these different entities. I recognized in the mid-seventies that the networking business was going through transformations due to the challenges offered by companies, such as MCI to AT&T, the nationwide communication network company at the time, and hence decided to work in that area. Of course, my basic training and projects at IIT Kharagpur and later at the University of Illinois had prepared me well to work in the networking field.

Bell Laboratories Data Networks (1976-1979)
In the Fall of 1976, I had an opportunity to join Bell Telephone Laboratories. I interviewed with three different groups and finally chose to join the Data Network Systems group, which was entrusted with the task of spearheading the development of a new digital network spanning throughout America and connecting all the digital devices: computers and terminals of different types and vendors. It was the largest project that AT&T or 'Ma Bell' as it was called then, had ever executed. There were teams from AT&T marketing working with the data systems development groups in Bell Laboratories. Western Electric had the task of manufacturing the hardware and the associated software, and then of installing the data networks and operating

them. This was the era before AT&T was divided into many pieces. Almost one million employees worked for AT&T at that time. A couple of thousand employees from different parts of the company were working on this project.

The Advanced Communication Service project was the most important project for AT&T to get into the data networking world and connect all the digital devices of the world by providing seamless communication service between them. It was too ambitious a project, and it saw IBM as the main eventual competition that was providing connectivity across all its computing elements.

The other urgency of introducing ACS across the United States was to enable all the different types of computer terminals to communicate with an intelligent network that would enhance their capabilities to communicate with disparate computers and other terminals by providing special terminal management services. So, AT&T marketing thought that there was a short period of a few years when an intelligent network could make those dumb terminals behave as intelligent terminals without upgrading or replacing them with intelligent terminals. Thus, AT&T would provide a nationwide intelligent data network connecting all the different types of terminals in service at the time to enhance their functionality. The backbone of the network was a packet-switching data network connecting all the computers and terminals.

As part of the systems engineering organization, I was in charge of defining the message service that was planned as the offering across the network.

The ACS project was the largest project that AT&T had ever undertaken and aimed to get into the computing world, entering from the communication end. The project had an estimated budget of about ten billion dollars, and that was a huge sum of money in the 1970s. Only Ma Bell could afford such a project! For the third year of my involvement in this project, I was also in charge of overall computer modeling of all the different components of project expenditure at AT&T Marketing, Ball Laboratories, and Western Electric. We then performed an Internal Rate of Return (IRR) analysis of the project to determine the viability against the projected revenue analysis.

As it turned out, the ACS project ran against the direction of technology. The cost of computing hardware was declining rapidly, and intelligent terminals and personal computers would soon proliferate in the world to replace the dumb terminals.

AT&T also underestimated the complexity of essentially a software project that embedded in it protocol conversion, mail, and message switching over the packet-switching data networks across the nation. I was disenchanted with the prospects of the project and left the data communication world to come back to the world of semiconductors at RCA Solid State Division in Somerville, NJ.

AT&T introduced ACS as part of their digital offerings in a limited edition in the New York area, and it was not very successful. This was before the days of the Netscape browser, which was developed at the University of Illinois, Urbana-Champaign, by Marc Andresen and colleagues. The web browser provided a simply defined interface software at the terminal end, opening the world of terminals to communicate with each other on a packet-switching network backbone without the complexity of distributed intelligence throughout the network, as was envisioned in the AT&T ACS project. Some of the people I worked with in these activities were Jim Arsenault, Chet McQuade, Pramod Verma, and many others.

DEC Personal Computer Networking (1991-1992)

After a break of almost twelve years working in the semiconductors and computers areas, I got back to working in the data networking area when I joined as a Senior Product Manager in the Personal Computer Networking Division of DEC at Littleton, Massachusetts.

It was an exciting opportunity, and for the first time, I was part of the marketing group defining the product requirements of personal computer networking software products. I was specifically in charge of the 'Pathworks for ULTRIX and SCO UNIX' products. The Pathworks family of products was a set of networking products provided by DEC to interconnect a varied set of personal computers running different operating system environments. Pathworks for ULTRIX was the networking software running on ULTRIX, the Unix version offered by DEC. Pathworks for SCO Unix was the networking software required to run on PCs running the Santa Cruz Operation (SCO) Unix operating system. I had to interface with the major customers running these network software products and their future needs in terms of the new product features needed or desired enhancements. The set of new requirements had to be first sanitized and prioritized, and then sent to the product design engineering group working on the particular product.

As the product marketing manager of the Pathworks products on SCO Unix, I remember attending the conference arranged by Santa Cruz Operation at Santa Cruz, CA, to find out their latest features in the coming offerings of their operating system. I moved around the country presenting the plans and features of DEC PC networking products. A video of the Pathworks for SCO Unix presentation by me was prepared in the marketing studio at DEC for use by the sales and customer support.

DEC had multiple families of personal computers of its own and a complex set of networking products to support all of the different personal computers that were commercially available. As they tried to consolidate and streamline the personal computer business, I left Digital Equipment Corporation and joined Process Software Corporation to head all of their engineering and technical publications departments.

Process Software Corporation (1993-1996)

I joined Process Software Corporation (PSC) of Framingham, Massachusetts, in the position of Director of Engineering in early 1993. Process Software was a small software company focusing on the development of networking software products for Digital Equipment Corporation's VAX VMS computer systems. A new development project was started to develop products related to Microsoft's Windows environment.

PSC decided to develop the first web server application to run on the Windows NT system. We licensed the core of such a server system that was developed at Edinburgh University, United Kingdom, and added further features to productize it. A web server, 'Purveyor', was developed and released in 1995, and it was the first available web server on the Windows NT Operating System. We marketed it for about a thousand dollars per copy and sold it in America and Europe. Microsoft Corporation also talked to us about this product, and we were interested in licensing or selling this product to them. But, after about six to nine months, Microsoft announced its Web Server product for Windows NT, and it was going to give it free to customers of Windows NT. This kind of made it tough for the Purveyor product to make a big impact in the market.

Process Software Corporation started with two entrepreneurs, Phil Denzer and Bernie Volz, at the Amherst campus of the University of Massachusetts, and then moved to Framingham, Massachusetts. It developed a stack of TCP/IP protocols for the VAX/VMS systems, and this was better than what was available from Digital Equipment Corporation. So, many customers of VAX/VMS systems all over the world used this. This was the main business of Process Software, and this brought a steady and increasing set of revenues. But they were now trying to diversify into other new areas, away from VAX/VMS systems. In that context, we introduced the Purveyor Web Server product for the Windows NT system after working on it for more than a year. I was also in charge of the technical publishing group that documented the software products developed at Process Software. It was a group of half a dozen writers and a manager/supervisor administering the personnel requirements to the different project schedules.

The other endeavor at Process Software was to develop a message server that would allow teamwork and joint development of documents. In that context, it would compete with Microsoft Exchange software product and similar ones from the other main players. Again, the target operating system for initial development was Windows NT.

Process Software Corporation was also looking for other new product areas to work on. I remember attending the discussions in early 1996 to target new projects. A couple of Search Engine companies had been coming up then in Massachusetts and elsewhere. One obvious gap at this time was the offering of search as a service, which Google and Yahoo later zeroed in, and became hugely successful. I was already in the process of moving from there, since I saw huge problems coming for the Purveyor business, and also for the new message server product, since Process Software was competing here against the giants and had only limited resources. I left Process Software in early 1996 to join Data General Corporation in Westborough.

10. World of Artificial Intelligence

Artificial Intelligence (AI) was introduced to me in 1970 when I entered the Digital Computer Laboratory to do my doctoral project. At the time, I audited a few courses in the area of artificial intelligence to prepare myself for working in the areas of advances happening in computer applications.

Artificial Intelligence has been around since the 1950s. The early work related to cybernetics, defined as 'the science of control and communication in the animal and machine' by Norbert Wiener. He is considered the father of cybernetics. As earlier reported in Chapter 4, my first exposure to this world was at the University of Illinois when I examined the problem of color vision in humans and its replication in machines.

The problem of test generation for different semiconductor integrated circuits was one task that was automated by the design of a generalized automated test program generator, and this was achieved during my experience at the RCA Solid State Division in Somerville, NJ. This was straightforward logic programming, and there was no artificial intelligence involved.

The problem of test generation becomes very complex in the case of generating test programs for new microprocessors and peripheral devices. I had the opportunity to deal with this problem during the years in the mid-eighties, when I was in charge of test generation for all the different microprocessors and peripheral devices procured from outside by Digital Equipment Corporation.

We developed a knowledge-based expert system for automated test generation of microprocessors and peripheral devices. It was an aggregate of expert systems within an expert system. Test vectors were generated at the functional block level, and this eliminates the need for gate-level diagrams. Each block-level expert system was a fully functional rule-based system and was equipped with knowledge for generating functional test vectors for generic functional blocks, such as RAM, ALU, etc. One could also design user-defined functional blocks. It was implemented in Knowledge Craft's CRL-OPS environment and incorporated into it about two hundred and sixty CRL-OPS rules. A technical paper detailing this special expert system called XTEST was presented at the Japan International Conference in 1987.

The development of expert systems for various specific applications was rampant in the eighties. Digital Equipment Corporation in Massachusetts had developed an expert system that automatically performed the system configuration as per the customer order, and this system, called XCON, was widely employed in the actual manufacturing environment.

Expert systems were also developed for specific financial applications, such as the design of insurance packages as per the specific customer background, stock market portfolio design, etc.

The key to the development of these expert systems was the capture of the knowledge from the leading experts. This knowledge was in the form of rules that the experts had learnt from their experience, and it was essential to capture this knowledge in terms of rules and then incorporate these into the expert systems. The AI systems at present are capable of learning from the data generated in various conditions of the systems, and developing the knowledge required for acting as an expert or an agent. This is a huge change from the eighties, when the development of such systems depended on the extraction of knowledge from the domain experts and then codifying that knowledge into rules to be incorporated into expert systems. The extraction of knowledge was a difficult and uneven process, and depended both on the domain experts and their interlocutors.

I had another opportunity to look at the development of expert systems when I worked at the Disk Subsystems group in Digital Equipment Corporation. There was a need for an expert system that could predict disk functional failures and performance degradations. Such an expert system could be used by the maintenance department to service the systems. Unfortunately, we never developed the knowledge, in terms of rules and data, that was required to develop such a system.

11. Move from America to India

It was always my plan from the very beginning to go back to India after a doctoral degree and work experience in the United States. Around the time of completion of the Ph.D. project, I had enquired about possible jobs in India in the electronics industry or as an academician. I had heard from IIT Delhi and ECIL (Electronics Corporation of India Ltd.) Hyderabad to contact them further. Since I got hired by Burroughs Corp under a training visa in June 1973, I did not pursue the possible openings in India at that time.

Since my main goal in life was to serve society by using my experience in electronics and computers, and to start some enterprise in the private sector, I steered my work career in the United States towards an eclectic mixture of work experience in product development rather than pure research.

As told earlier, I had looked at the possibility of establishing a semiconductor test and assembly facility in India in 1986, and then moving my family back to India. That was supposed to be an entrepreneurship, with a partner. But that was not deemed possible at that time, and I also realized that it was not always possible to have a compatible business partner. So, I had to go solo if I wanted to move to India. In early 1987, I visited India to look firsthand at the business environment in India. Later in 1987, I also explored the possibility of taking up an engineering assignment as a director in

India for a small American CAD Software company that had established operations in India. After getting the offer and looking at the tone of the offer letter and reporting structure, I realized that it would not work out. At that point, I decided that I would go back to India to start a company along with my wife, and that we had to make financial and other arrangements for that. One key requirement was to have a residence of your own that could provide you necessary comforts and facilities you want, and would be a stabilizing factor during a new venture. From the timing point of view, it would be nice to move to India around 1992, when my son Arun would be eleven years old. So, I embarked on a plan to get the residence ready for the purpose and then have a financial plan to sustain life even in the worst case.

For one to make a move back to India after a working career in the United States for a dozen years or more, one must decide for sure that they want to move. In the context of making a move, one has to figure out the provisions for the financial requirements and a residence. Although owning a residence is not essential to a move, having one allows you to cultivate a feeling of belonging and continuity in the transition process. Since completing a residence takes anywhere from two to five years in India, the family gets the chance to visit and stay at the future residence before the actual move.

As far as the timing eventual move, it has to be synchronized with the academic development of the children. In my case, I first thought of a move when my son was just five years old in the year 1986, since it would be easy for my son to make a transition to the Indian school system. Another timeframe is when the child starts attending middle school.

Choosing an Indian City

It was in 1987 that I finally took some concrete steps towards making a move back to India. I took a trip to India in January 1987 to assess firsthand the environment in India, especially eastern India, as far as industrial prospects and the support structure for raising a young family. My preference at the time was to start some enterprise around Kolkata or Bhubaneswar. My in-laws lived all their lives in the center of South Kolkata, and hence, I could count on some family and societal support around Kolkata.

I had given advance to purchase a plot of land in the Salt Lake area earlier, and after further enquiry, found that the plot was in an area completely remote and undeveloped. So, I canceled to purchase plot in Salt Lake. One cannot just build a house in the middle of nowhere and move a young family from the United States to that place. So, I focused on looking at some plots within the city itself. I considered the possibility of buying a developed residential house in the Salt Lake area. I was finally discouraged from buying a residential property because of the property laws around Kolkata, and learning about the use of muscle and political power for the harassment of property owners when the property is rented out.

I took a trip to Bhubaneswar from Kolkata along with my father-in-law and stayed for a couple of days at Saheed Nagar at the residence of the eldest daughter of Sadananda Rath, a retired Income Tax Commissioner and a friend of my father-in-law. I had a meeting with an officer in charge of the nodal agency, IPICOL of the Government of Odisha, Saheed Nagar. I was apprised of the various schemes that the government had to aid new enterprises in the engineering and manufacturing areas.

From various information sources, I also came to

know how a start was made in the electronics area in Odisha by State Government units that designed, manufactured, and sold the television brand 'Konark TV' and how some of these manufacturing efforts had come to a closure due to mismanagement and a non-competitive product cost environment because of a lack of a mass manufacturing process. In addition, there were complex labor and union problems in electronics manufacturing organizations that impeded automation and mass manufacturing. I was convinced at the end of the trip to Odisha that planning any electronics manufacturing operation in Odisha was not a good prospect at the time, considering the lack of an ecosystem of electronics manufacturing.

I had long ago visited Bhubaneswar in 1968 when I took a trip along with my classmates from IIT Kharagpur to show them Puri, Konark, Bhubaneswar, and Cuttack. Bhubaneswar, in the meantime, had become a well-planned capital city of Odisha and certainly showed much future promise to be the main city of Odisha. I decided in my mind that I would plan to have a residence in Bhubaneswar and also look for a career opportunity anywhere in India in the meantime.

I had stayed in Bengaluru for a couple of months during my summer training at Bharat Electronics in 1967 and liked it as a neat garden city where one could live with a job in the electronics industry. But I thought Bengaluru was too far from Odisha, where most of my relatives lived. If I started an operation myself, it had to be in Bhubaneswar, and hence, a residence there would be the first step toward a move to India. I did look around the suburbs of Delhi too, especially Dwarka, Gurugram, and Noida. Although I liked Delhi as a great city providing a wide variety of opportunities as the capital city of India, it was too far from

Odisha to have a residence there. So finally, it was decided that we would look for a plot or a finished or unfinished house in Bhubaneswar.

Building a Residence in India

We came upon a half-built house near the main artery of Bhubaneswar. It belonged to a Bengali family, and after further enquiry in Kolkata, we found that it was not available for sale anymore. We looked at a member of private plots in Bhubaneswar, and most of them had problems of access and uncertainty about the surrounding development. So, we decided to look for a plot allotted by the government in any planned township under Bhubaneswar. My father-in-law searched for a plot for us and was able to make a deal to buy a plot size 60ft x 90ft allotted to a politician right in front of the largest park in Bhubaneswar. During this process, he was enticed to buy for himself a smaller plot of size 50ft x 75ft at the corner of a main road so that he could build a house in Bhubaneswar and possibly move from the apartment in Kolkata, where he had lived since the 1940s. Ironically, the Government of Odisha had allotted him a large plot of size, about 110'x100' in the 1960s in central Bhubaneswar, and he asked me once if I would be interested in owning this plot. At the time, I was not aware of the housing plot sizes in India and did not show interest, thinking that it was a small plot. He gave that plot away to a distant relative, famous singer Prafulla Kar, since he did not want to invest any money in building a house! Most people in India acquire and build properties to live in and obtain some long-term returns in terms of appreciation of the land and building. Since the rental return per annum of a property is only one to two percent, it is always much cheaper to rent rather than own a property. Of course, there was not much land appreciation in the 1960s and the 1970s, and hence people did not go for real estate investment.

Once my father-in-law bought the small corner lot for himself and made plans to construct a building on that, he realized that whatever money he had would be exhausted in building that house, and decided not to build, but wanted us to build his house with the provision that he would pass on the title of the property to my wife. So, we had two plots in Bhubaneswar where we could build the houses for our eventual return from the United States!

I transferred a sum of $40,000/- to my NRE account at Kolkata Ballygunge SBI so that the construction work could start on both of the plots. To transfer the ownership, the ground-floor house had to be built as per plan, and then only the government allowed the transfer of the plots.

We decided to first complete the building on the plot, owned by my father-in-law, since it was on the corner of two main roads and had more commercial opportunities there. This building at N3-B6, IRC Village, was planned such that one to five families can live there with independent entries. It was designed as two adjacent three-floor buildings, each with its separate roof castings and stairs, but connected with the other by doors near the stairs. I had planned the layout after modifying the one my father-in-law had.

The N3-B6 IRC Village house ground floor superstructure was completed in December 1989, two years after we had acquired the plot and about a year after we started the construction. During this construction period, my in-laws lived in a rented house close by. We finished two of the rooms on the ground floor of the smaller building of plinth size 25'x25', and it was three feet below the level of the main building. This was like the basement level, being at the same level as the main road on one side.

A Pratishtha ceremony was done in December 1989, and my in-laws moved there from the rented house. I visited Bhubaneswar at the time, along with my wife and son, and stayed there for a couple of weeks. Our acclimatization with Bhubaneswar had started. From then on, we visited India and Bhubaneswar almost every year during summer vacation in August or September timeframe, or during the December school vacation.

By the end of 1992, the complete building infrastructure of the three floors was completed. In addition, the ground floor of the main building was finished along with the mezzanine first floor of the adjacent building. All in all, three bathrooms and six possible bedrooms were finished to provide ample living space for the family. Adjacent to the building on the side of the main road was government-owned land measuring about 60' wide between the road and our boundary wall that was available to develop a garden of about 2500 sq ft. Two dozen mango, coconut, guava, Lichi, banana, pomegranate, and other fruit trees were planted, and the lawn was developed to give a very welcome green cover around the whole building. The building, along with the adjacent garden developed by us at government land, became one of the main attractive features of this building. For future road expansion, the government would utilize ten to fifteen feet of the land, but most of it would be available for us as a garden since all of the houses on this side were given access to the main road through this government land. It could not be allocated to someone else as a separate plot for building a house on it.

The larger land plot was ideally located in front of the Ekamrakanan Gardens, the largest garden of about two hundred acres, adjoining the jungle land where the elephants often roamed. Our plot was in the middle of a large block with a very wide road with space for sidewalks. There was a piece of land about 100 feet wide intervening between the road and the gardens, and this was later on developed into a long walking park spanning the complete block of houses. This walking park was named after the famous Odia singer Akshaya Mohanty.

We designed this house to be our eventual dream house to live there, away from the road noise. The ground floor of this house was completed around the year 1992 with the guidance of an executive engineer friend, Gopal Brahma. The transfer of the plot to Anuradha was made after the completion of the ground-floor infrastructure. The doors and windows had to be made and installed, although plumbing, electrical work, and finishing were not done. Once the transfer was done, the work on this house was stopped, waiting for us to come back and decide on the next step.

Timing the Move

Although I had estimated that the eventual move to India would take five years and that I would move to India in 1992, the eventual move took another five years. In the middle of the year 1995, we decided that we had to make the move by the middle of 1997.

My son was in the tenth grade in high school in the United States. So, he would be able to join the Plus 2 program in Indian colleges, where the eleventh and twelfth grades were taught in colleges. Since he could choose 'Alternate English' as his language choice instead of any Indian vernacular language, it would be easy for him.

We wanted to see Europe before moving to India and planned a trip starting from London. We saw the main attractions London offered, such as Trafalgar Square, the

Parliament Building, Buckingham Palace, and museums. We also took trips to see some of the castles and forts outside of London, such as Windsor Castle. From London, we got on a steamer as part of a travel group and crossed the English Channel, and arrived in Belgium. We started the bus tour along with this group and stopped for a night in Brussels. After looking through the main tourist attractions in the city square, we drove to the city of Geneva in Switzerland. We stayed there for a couple of days, visiting the lakes and business districts. We then drove to Venice, Florence, and Rome in Italy, spending a day each there and looking at all the beautiful buildings and statues. From Rome, we went through Pisa and looked at the Leaning Tower of Pisa, and then went to Monaco to spend a night there. The next destination was Paris, where we spent two days looking at the Versailles Palace, the Eiffel Tower, Museum, and the restaurants in the city. We had our farewell dinner with the group and left the following day to get back to London, and then fly back to the United States. It was a very educational trip for all of us, especially Arun. We had seen the magnificence of European civilization! We were getting ready mentally to move back to India.

Before we moved, we had to make sure that Arun's future education and career were enhanced by moving to India. Arun came home one day after school in seventh grade and told us that he would like to be a 'psychologist' since he likes to talk with people and listen to their problems. Of course, I had my idea that he would perhaps study economics, literature, journalism, and any area except engineering. Although I felt that psychology may not be the right career path for him, I was glad that he had a vision and tried to encourage him to go after his dream! So, he decided to have one of the optional subjects as psychology.

In the Indian system at the leading college in Bhubaneswar, the only choice for him was to study Plus 2 Arts and take psychology as one of the subjects. It was not possible for him to study Plus 2 Science and take psychology as one of the four subjects. So, it was decided that he would study Plus 2 Arts with Psychology, Mathematics, Logic, and Sociology as his optional subjects. So, Arun was admitted to Buxi Jagabandhu Bidyadhar (BJB) College in July 1997 and stayed with his grandmother at our house in Bhubaneswar. I went back to the United States after a few weeks to wind down our affairs at Westborough, MA. Anuradha was still working at Digital Equipment Corporation as a Senior Finance Manager in their Storage Systems Group. She resigned from her position. We shipped all the furniture and other personal belongings in a container to be shipped to India. Anuradha left for India and joined her mother and Arun at Bhubaneswar. I stayed back to sell the house. Once it was sold, I emptied the house, taking the few things that we had kept for our townhouse condominium in Fall River, MA.

A few years earlier, we had purchased a building in Fall River, which had three townhouses side by side. We had them all rented. I had kept the biggest of these townhouses empty and free for our use by not renewing the rental agreement once it expired. So, I moved along with whatever was left in the house at Westborough, enough furniture and utilities for use in this two-bedroom townhouse. Thus, we had a place in Fall River to stay as we visited the United States. We also kept a car in the parking lot in front of our townhouse for use whenever we stayed there. We had completed the move of the family to India.

Part III
Work Years in India
(1997 to 2010)

12. PanNet Computer
13. World of Technical Education
14. A Miraculous Escape
15. Life During Work Years in India

12. PanNet Computer

Company Formation and First Year

I flew to India in January of 1997 to get things ready for the move of the family to Bhubaneswar and to start the company there as per my vision at the time. The N3-B6 IRC Village house had been completed except for the finishing of the top floors. My mother-in-law had been living in this house for some years, waiting for us to move there.

The plan was to complete the flooring and plastering of the top floors so that the whole building would be available for us to live there by the middle of the year. Accordingly, marble flooring of the first floor was completed along with the two bathrooms on this floor. The complete house had five bathrooms and plenty of bedrooms on each floor to house us and our in-laws, and would still have additional rooms for commercial use if needed.

I traveled every morning to the office of OSEDC (Odisha State Electronics Development Corporation), which was situated in Saheed Nagar, the commercial center of Bhubaneswar. OSEDC was supposed to help me start the process of establishing the company in Bhubaneswar. With the help of a Chartered Accountant, the company PanNet Computer Pvt. Ltd. was registered with its registered address at N3-B6, IRC Village, Nayapally, Bhubaneswar-15. The intention was to establish a company that engaged in computer software, networking, computer systems services, computer applications, and training. In other words, I wanted to provide products and services in

Bhubaneswar and the surrounding areas in eastern India that were needed by the customers. If we could satisfy the needs of the customers, then real-world software solutions may come out of that effort!

As part of the preparatory work, an application was made to the Government of Odisha for establishing a software development and service company. PanNet Computer (P) Ltd. was registered on 1st April 1997, having its registered office at N3-B6, IRC Village, Bhubaneswar-751015. Orissa State Electronics Development Corporation (OSEDC) signed a memorandum of understanding to make an equity investment and offer a venture capital loan to PanNet.

PanNet's mission was to provide software development services to clients in India and abroad, and also to develop complete hardware and software solutions as needed by customers in India. In addition, PanNet intended to provide specialized training services for computer professionals.

PanNet set up a software development center at the Software Technology Park (STP) established by the Government of India at Bhubaneswar. PanNet got the approval of the Foreign Investment Promotion Board (FIPB) to export software from this unit established at the STP Bhubaneswar. PanNet Computer (P) Ltd. operated as a subsidiary of PanNet Corporation of the United States. PanNet Computer (P) Ltd. also signed a memorandum of understanding with Orissa State Electronics Development Corporation (OSEDC), whereby the latter offered to make an equity investment and offered to grant a venture capital loan.

In addition to the facility set up at the Software Technology Park, PanNet established the Systems and Administrative Center on one side of the N3-B6, IRC

Village building in Bhubaneswar, just about half a km from the STP site. After a few months of operation at the STP site, it was decided to merge the STP operation of PanNet with the center at the N3-B6 building. This was done by installing the antenna at the building to connect with the STP network for the internet.

Moving to India from the United States, one of my priorities was to arrange life such that there was a minimum amount of hustle relating to commuting and other regular daily activities. Since I did not find the government-managed Software Technology Park to have the proper environment, I moved the complete business operation of PanNet Computer to my house in the IRC Village.

The house at IRC Village was designed as two separate buildings with independent entries and connected next to the second set of stairs in the side building. Hence, there was no problem having the company operate from the side building, separate from the living quarters. We had to just add an iron set of stairs on the outside of the side building so that one can go from the ground floor to the second floor. The second-floor large room was being used as the engineering area where six to ten engineers could work, isolated from other activities on the bottom two floors of the company. We also converted the garage room to an enclosed office room and added a bathroom to the attached outhouse, and made that into a reception room for the company.

After making the registration of PanNet and upgrading the house in Bhubaneswar, I went back to the United States to bring my son to India so that he could get admitted to BJB College in the July/August timeframe. In the meantime, I had applied and received an equivalent certificate from an organization in New Delhi that Arun's completing the tenth grade in Massachusetts was equivalent to passing the tenth-grade examination in India. So, Arun became eligible for admission into the Plus 2 arts stream in India. With the help of M.S. Das of OSEDC, we were able to get admission into the Plus2 arts stream. Of course, he scored in the nineties in terms of total points based on his school grades and extra credit for tennis. I purchased a Maruti Omni car that could be used for personal and company purposes, especially since it could provide transport for eight or more persons. Since BJB College was about six to seven km from our house, our driver could drop off and pick up Arun from the college. After hiring some of the first engineers at PanNet and defining the immediate projects, I went back to the United States to wind up things at Westborough, MA. We packed most of our belongings and sent them by sea to Kolkata. Anuradha resigned from her job at DEC and left for India. I waited in Westborough to complete the sale of the house. Once that happened, I moved alone to our townhouse in Fall River, MA. I stayed there trying to arrange business for PanNet Computer from the USA and Canada.

The shipments from Westborough in October 1997 finally arrived in Kolkata in December, and we were notified in Bhubaneswar about that. Anuradha went to Kolkata and got all the stuff released from the customs office there, and got all the things loaded in trucks and brought to Bhubaneswar. Fortunately, the customs officer was an Odia officer known to my brother-in-law, Pratap Pathy of Kolkata, and he did not charge us any customs duty. Of course, we had only stuff that we had used at our house in Westborough, and now for use only at our residence in Bhubaneswar

After the year 1997-1998, the first full year of operation

of PanNet, projects in five different areas were started based upon the local requirements as determined by surveying the business environments in Bhubaneswar:
1. Multimedia Product Development
2. Computer Systems and Networking Services
3. Software Training Products and Services
4. Pattern Recognition and AI Products and Services
5. ERP Software Products and Services

All of these technical projects were simultaneously started during the year as the engineers were hired into the company. In addition, the company management explored the possibility of obtaining software maintenance and development contracts in the United States of America.

Multimedia Product Developments

This was one of the first areas where we started developing products, one of the reasons being, the first engineer who was hired into PanNet had a good background in this area, and there were some local needs at the time. At that time, there was no commercially available Compact Disc (CD) that focused on Odisha and its culture and tourist attractions around the state. So, after a few weeks of market research, it was decided that a CD would be prepared by the company to include all such relevant information on Odisha. This would be the first product of the company and would be called 'The Land of Black Krishna' (TLBK), the English translation of the Odia title, 'Kalia Kahnura Desha'. The highest deity of Odisha, Jagannath, is also known as the 'Kalia Kanhu' or the 'Black Krishna'.

This CD was released in 1999 and sold in India and abroad. The product used the latest multimedia tool, Director, to organize all the information on Odisha. As part of the effort to survey the latest tools and technologies, I attended the Multimedia conference near San Francisco, in October 1997, where Steve Jobs of Apple Inc. delivered a special speech on how he was aiming to change the world through technology.

We also planned to develop other CD products on the most important verses of the Bhagavad Gita and the life story of the Buddha.

An internet site, 'OrissaOL' for online information on Odisha, was developed by including important information relevant to tourists and others.

An effort was also made to develop animation products to be marketed all over the world. The first such story chosen was that of Dharama, the son of the chief artisan who built the temple at Konark in the thirteenth century during the rule of Odisha King Narasingha Deva. He had never seen his father since he was born after his father left to build the temple twelve years ago. Dharama eventually helped to install the head structure of the temple and sacrificed his own life. An artist was hired from the BK School of Arts in Bhubaneswar to draw pictures of Dharama at different positions so that animation scenes could be developed.

All of these projects in the area of multimedia product development were stopped in the year 2000 when we did not receive as much market demand as we anticipated from the product sales of TLBK. We also decided that this was a diversion from our main focus area of software development, and hence, no more efforts should be focused on this area except for marketing TLBK as opportunities arose.

Computer and Networking Services

At the time of shipping our belongings through a

container by sea, I had also packaged and sent the Dell server that I had bought in 1996, along with the desktop personal computers and a CISCO Router we had. We also needed to procure a dozen or more desk PCs for the engineers. During the process of searching for computer vendors selling and maintaining personal computer systems in Bhubaneswar, we realized that there was a need to provide such services in the local market. So, we became a distributor of PCs for a PC manufacturer in Eastern India. But we soon realized that there were plenty of under-the-table dealings in the procurement deals and decided not to distribute computer systems. However, PanNet continued to provide network design and installation services for customers who procured their computers and depended upon the outside vendor for setting up and maintaining the network.

Training Products and Services

There was a great need in the years nineteen nineties for training school and college graduates in the latest software technology to make them employable. A good number of computer software training companies started at this time in India. PanNet was also pushed in this direction to provide these needed services without being a franchise of any of the training service companies. PanNet developed a set of courses on C Programming, Java, HTML, Oracle Database, and e-commerce applications. These courses drew hundreds of students to take the training. PanNet Institute awarded them course certificates and special diploma programs after the completion of a series of courses.

The software training courses were regularly updated and offered to the students. Many of the engineering students also did their Bachelor's degree required projects in the final year at PanNet. There was an opportunity at the time to scale up those efforts and extend the training services to other towns in Odisha and elsewhere through the franchise arrangement.

Though the training services produced enough revenue to sustain the salaries of the teachers and the course developers, it did not produce any gross profit to continuously enhance the systems and networks or take care of other administrative and general expenses. This was due to the following reasons. The course fees were extremely competitive to keep pace with other training joints springing up around the Bhubaneswar area. However, we provided a thorough course as per the outline promised, and it always took much more time than the allocated time for the course. Hence, the company rarely made any profit through these training service endeavors. Towards the end of 2006, it was decided to close these efforts as we needed to upgrade the computer systems and software.

Pattern Recognition and AI Products

One of PanNet's customers in Bhubaneswar, CTTC (Central Tools Room & Technology Centre), asked us if we could provide them automatic grading software solution for examinations they conducted every year to select the trainees for their courses. As a central government-funded organization, they are required to test the capabilities of the aspirants from the answers to about a hundred objective questions with yes/no answers. We designed a software program, written in C, that counted the dark pixels in the designated circles for the correct yes/no answers shown in answer sheets. A roll number was also incorporated into the answer sheets for the examinee to write this filling up the correct ovals in pencil or pen. The answer sheets were scanned on the system automatically, and the answers were evaluated, and came up with the tabulation of marks as per the sequential roll numbers. This software was developed along with a simplified user interface and delivered to the customer in the year 2000.

During the year 2001, there came a need to automate the Joint Entrance Examination for engineering students for admission to the different engineering colleges in the state of Odisha. PanNet was requested to offer a solution and conduct these tests to be performed as part of the Orissa JEE 2002. PanNet developed a solution and successfully performed the automatic evaluation of the test results. Subsequently, PanNet performed the automatic evaluation of test results for many organizations in Odisha and the neighboring states in eastern India.

During the year 2006, Kalinga Institute of Industrial Technology (KIIT) University wanted to automate the entrance test that was being performed all over India, and PanNet was roped in for the test conducted in 2006.

PanNet also successfully conducted the KIIT Entrance tests during the year 2007. To conduct these tests, PanNet had procured special high-speed scanners that could allow us to have the test results within days of having collected all the test sheets from the test centers.

PanNet also sold a version of the generalized test examination software (PanNet ExamPro) to a limited number of institutions that had to hold their test and evaluations outside the Bhubaneswar area.

The above pattern recognition product for the automatic grading of examination answer sheets was the most profitable product developed by PanNet and was used for more than a decade. It is perhaps still being used in organizations like CTTC, which had licensed copies. PanNet had obtained character recognition software, both for printed text and cursive writing, to extend our capabilities for non-examination applications, such as fingerprint verification for police. But we could not land on a defined requirement for such an application from the police authorities in Bhubaneswar or Kolkata.

One of the last projects undertaken at PanNet was for an artificial intelligence (AI) application for public health purposes. The idea was that we could ask a few questions to rural folks regarding their heart health, and by analyzing their answers to these questions, we could determine who needs further detailed analysis and treatment. A neural network-based system could be developed to analyze the answers and other patient data, and then come up with the results of the diagnosis.

The development strategy was to first duplicate the heart disease diagnostic expert system developed at a university in Turkiye that had identified eleven input attributes and the forty-four rule base to generate an output that would identify the level of heart problem. It was to be implemented in MATLAB from MathWorks along with the Fuzzy Logic Toolbox. This was the very last project started at PanNet in the year 2010 and was terminated at the closure of PanNet.

ERP Products and Services

PanNet intended to develop software solutions for the companies operating in India, especially in eastern India, with the hope that some of these could be later developed into generalized software products that would be sold to customers. In that regard, we had obtained the latest Oracle-based database software and wanted to develop specific applications for customers.

Materials Management System

Paradeep Phosphates Limited (PPL) was a fertilizer company in the port town of Paradip, about one hundred km from Bhubaneswar. Although they had a liaison office in Bhubaneswar, their main operation and administration offices were in Paradip. PPL requested us to provide an automation solution to their materials handling problems. PanNet proposed the custom development of a materials management program based on the Oracle Database system. PanNet signed a contract with them in the year 1999 to develop and deliver the software solution. It was to be delivered early in the year 2000, working along with the Paradip operation. The super-cyclone of October 1999 in Odisha had major disruptions at the PPL operation in Paradip, and their office premises were inundated with water for days. Regardless of these difficulties, we delivered a solution to the materials management problem in the year 2000 to their satisfaction. It was installed and used by the personnel at PPL.

PPL was later acquired by the Zuari group, and soon thereafter, PPL adopted the ERP system used by Zuari as part of the integration process. We lost a valued customer in the process.

We wanted to generalize this materials management software product for usage by various industries, but could not muster together the marketing strategy and the finances to develop this.

Railways Applications

The signaling department in the Railways had quite a few needs to automate their operations, and we worked with them for almost two to three years in defining and prototyping software products for them. However, there was no order or any revenue from these efforts.

College Management Systems

PanNet developed a version of college management systems in the year 2002 to help educational institutions manage their operations more efficiently. This was marketed to a few educational institutions in eastern India. Rajendra College in Balangir had obtained an early version of this product, but did not use it sufficiently to automate their operation.

Textile Applications

PanNet opened an office in Kolkata in the year 2004 to explore the business opportunities in the Kolkata metropolitan area. An office was opened on the third floor of the building situated at the corner of Gariahat Road and Rash Behari Avenue. A full-time marketing manager was hired to identify customers requiring support to streamline their operations. One such customer was a manufacturing company that was engaged in the production of garments. We analyzed their complete manufacturing process to design a custom ERP application for them. However, the project was finally halted when it did not result in a concrete customer order.

Pharmaceutical Applications

We had spent quite a bit of time defining a set of ERP applications for the pharmaceutical industry at the request of an organization in the Kolkata area. We terminated this project in the absence of concrete customer requirements.

Restructuring PanNet Computer

It was evident to me from the very beginning that we entered into too many different segments of business related to computer hardware and software. One reason was that we did not know what the market needs were and what would succeed within the business environment that was manageable for us. The first business that was closed was the multimedia product and service business, and it was closed in the year 2000.

Computer hardware and the networking hardware and services business were closed in the year 2003, since we could not do any under-the-table deals to get contracts.

Software training services were closed in the year 2006 since we could not compete to profitably provide the level of services as desired by us.

Because of the closure of the above businesses, we were left only with software development services and had to terminate the employees engaged in other services. The company was using the three floors of the side building at IRC Village, and was using the adjoining two rooms on the ground and the first floor of the main building as a conference room and executive office as needed. The company did not need all this space and kept only the large engineering room on the second floor and the two small rooms on the ground floor, along with the bathroom for all the other needs. The rest of the building was rented out by us to a Real Estate Development Company, which used the whole building as its headquarters. We moved from the residential side to our new home in the VIP Colony, a block away.

The ERP applications business that we focused on for software development did not succeed due to the difficulty of getting many concrete customer commitments beyond the initial requirements phases. The examination services business slowly died down because most of the customers wanted to conduct these tests themselves so that they would have control over the results. Some customers also moved to the online computer testing process.

In the year 2010, we finally closed the company and rented the rest of the building to the real estate development company. We kept only two rooms on the ground floor of the side building, along with the bathroom, for our use in the different social experimental projects we wanted to execute during our retirement years.

We worked with many people during the fourteen years PanNet was in operation. Some of them are Rashesh Patnaik, Mahesh Patnaik, Mrinal Mohanty, Sonali Dutta, Nirmalya Sinha, Himansu, Suresh, Surabhi, and many other employees.

13. World of Technical Education

There was a big demand for engineering education in Odisha around the time I came back from the USA and started PanNet at Bhubaneswar. Many of the software training companies also started engineering colleges around this time, and hence, I wanted to explore opportunities in this area. To explore this, I registered PanNet Foundation Trust in May 2001 to offer engineering and other educational services as a non-profit organization. I was the chairman of the trust, and there were three other directors, one of them being my wife, Anuradha.

At least a dozen engineering colleges had already started at this time around Bhubaneswar, and each of them was fervently developing new engineering campuses and adding new branches of engineering, or increasing the seat capacities. Each institute required a minimum of ten acres of land to start with, if multiple engineering branches were to be added. I wanted to cautiously tread this path since it would be a huge undertaking to start and sustain a world-class engineering college in Odisha with transparent funding and management. We got the application for starting the Master's in Computer Applications (MCA) program since it required a limited set of land, buildings, and staff, and could be started by renting the facilities available at our disposal in Bhubaneswar. MCA was a six-semester program that was open to anyone with a Bachelor's degree with Mathematics as one of the subjects in the twelfth grade, and later.

Later that summer in 2001, I went to the USA and stayed at my townhouse condominium at Lewin Street in Fall River, Massachusetts. It was customary for me to visit the United States of America at least once every year. It was a September morning, and I was logged into the internet to look at the latest news in my basement study room. The incredible fury of 9/11 was in front of my eyes for the next couple of hours. I returned to India later that September, and everyone was asking me about that historic destruction in the heart of New York.

Barapada Institute of Engineering and Technology

A couple of my friends, who had earlier that year wanted to collaborate with me to start the MCA program in Bhubaneswar, asked me if I could be available to become the principal of a large private engineering college in the Bhadrak area in North Odisha. It was an interesting proposition. I could live in Bhubaneswar and drive to Barapda in the outskirts of Bhadrak township every week, and live there at the quarters for the principal during the week, and drive back during the weekend.

They would provide a car with a driver to be at my service. A cook and caretaker would be there at the principal's quarters to take care of my needs during the week.

Anuradha was already taking care of the matters relating to the operation of PanNet Computer when I was absent during my long jaunts to the United States of America, and I was always available through the phone and the internet. Often, we conducted phone and chat interviews for the candidates being hired into the company.

As always, I was ready to help if it was going to be beneficial to the state of engineering education in northern

Odisha. It was going to be a new adventure into the quagmire of managing private engineering colleges at the time. Barapada Institute of Engineering Technology (BIET) was an established engineering college that started decades earlier as a diploma engineering institute and had extended its programs more recently to include all major engineering degree branches. It had also started MCA and MBA programs, and had somewhat dormant Industrial Training Institute (ITI) programs for imparting specific skills to high school students. BIET had a campus of more than eighty acres of land on the outskirts of Bhadrak and attracted students from all over Odisha and the neighboring eastern states of Jharkhand, Bihar, and West Bengal.

I joined the college as the Principal in October of 2002 and stayed in Barapada at the Principal's quarters. The college was being managed by a Board of Governors, of which the principal was a member. The secretary of the Board was a senior teaching staff, who belonged to the Bhadrak area. The chairman of the board was the local MLA, Prafulla Samal, and there were members with political and social connections in that area.

There were many immediate challenges at the college:
1. This was the time in 2001 when there was a wide retrenchment in the employment of engineers in India and Western countries, and hence there was less demand for entering engineering. So, we needed to attract a sufficient number of students to fill the sanctioned capacities in the engineering and diploma programs. The placement of graduates was miserable, and it was almost disastrous for the diploma holders.
2. New teaching staff had to be recruited for the vacant positions in the departments of Electronics, Computer Science, and others.

3. The engineering laboratories needed to be properly maintained and enhanced with the latest equipment. The computer systems laboratories and the networking infrastructure had to be put in place.
4. There was an attendance problem with many of the teaching staff, and classes were not regularly held, especially in diploma-level courses. There was a general management problem with all the academic and non-academic staff.
5. A new academic building was being planned to provide a better academic environment. New hostel buildings were being built to accommodate more of the female students. The certification audits were going on for the different academic programs. New applications were being submitted for starting the business administration programs and MCA programs.
6. There were the perennial problems of holding the examination scheduled by the university without copying and unfair practices.

In summary, there was a continuous set of problems to be solved on a day-to-day and long-term basis. The last principal was there only for a short period. Before that, one of the senior retired professors of mechanical engineering from IIT Kharagpur was there as the principal for a couple of years.

I worked at the principal's office in the Administrative Block from the morning to the evening, except for the lunch break when I went to the Principal's Quarters for lunch. There were meetings, often in the evening, at the residence with members of the Board of Governors and the Chairman. I used to leave for Bhubaneswar on Saturday mornings or Friday evenings and then drive back to

Barapada on Monday mornings. Even at Bhubaneswar, there were meetings relating to issues relating to various administrative and long-term issues.

It was a very busy schedule for me at BIET in the first couple of months. Hence, I decided to stay at the Principal's Quarters even during the weekends so that no issues requiring my attention were dropped due to my absence during the weekend, especially issues relating to the residential hostels.

Later that year, there were many issues relating to the conduct of University examinations in the college. I communicated to everyone that copying was an absolute no-no, and there would be strict invigilation of the examinations. There was a demand from a section of students for the management not to take any action against any malpractice because the teachers had not taught all the required topics and had not prepared the students properly to face the examinations. I repeatedly clarified that there would not be any malpractice during the examinations. The university examinations for the third-year students started with the appropriate planning. The examinations were being conducted smoothly. On the last day of the examination, I went to check the examination hall as usual in the middle of the examination period. Everything was fine, and there was no visible malpractice. I came back to my office and was waiting for the particular examination to conclude. I learned that a particular student taking the examination stood up just fifteen minutes before the end of the examination, and made a big splash for the students to abandon the examination and walk out of the hall. So, that happened, and the students came around to the principal's office and 'gheraoed' me. Immediately, I called the local police to come and support me. I was in the principal's office along with staff members, and we had bolted our door from the inside so that no one could enter the office. After some discussions with some of the staff members after the arrival of the police personnel, I decided to call sine die at the third-year hostel facilities so that the students had to go back to their hometowns, and there would not be any disturbance from this batch of students. Later that day, I went to the Police station and lodged the FIR (First Information Report) of the whole incident. There was no further turmoil thereafter since the particular batch of students started leaving due to the closure of the hostel. Thus, we avoided what could have been ugly and uncontrolled mass student hysteria! The incident did not help anyone and rather hindered the particular batch of students since that particular subject examination had to be canceled, and hence they had to take the examination again sometime in the future when it took place. I was happy that I could stick to my principle of not allowing any malpractice, but I was perturbed by the student power against it.

The college was closed for the Christmas vacation. I visited Chennai along with Anuradha and Arun, who flew from the United States during the semester break at the University of Illinois. After the vacation, I informed the management at BIET that I was resigning from my position as Principal. Thus ended a very brief but eventful set of months in managing a private engineering college. I learned a great deal about how such private educational institutes are supported and managed, and the problems and politics associated. I kept up the relations with BIET thereafter by being a member of the board of governors of BIET for a few years after my resignation.

Biju Patnaik National Steel Institute

Around the time of upheaval at BIET in December 2001, I was contacted by some friends if I could join a new organization that the Government of India was starting, along with the Government of Odisha, to impart the latest technological requirements relating to the steel industry. I was called for a quick interview in Delhi, where I met the IAS officers in charge of the Ministry of Steel and the Minister of Steel. Things moved very fast, and I joined the newly started Biju Patnaik National Steel Institute (BPNSI) in January 2002. Thus ended my brief but tumultuous Journey through the labyrinth of the private engineering education industry.

Biju Patnaik National Steel Institute (BPNSI) was envisioned as a leading teaching and technology development organization to steer the steel industry in India. The Minister of Steel decided to establish this institute in Puri town, and a prime building on the beach was rented to start the Institute. It earlier belonged to the royal family of Nepal, but was acquired by Odisha Tourism Development and managed as a hotel. The building was completely refurbished inside to include mid-size classrooms, offices, and laboratories. The refurbishment was completed on a fast track, and the institute was inaugurated by the Chief Minister of Odisha in the first week of January 2002 in a gala ceremony on the front of the institute overlooking the Bay of Bengal.

BPNSI was started with support from the Ministry of Steel to be an educational institute for developing specialized and trained personnel required by the steel industry, and also to be a center for steel technology development. We started with two streams of diploma programs: 1. Diploma in Steel Technology for anyone with a B.Sc. degree, and 2.

the Diploma in Information Technology for anyone with a Bachelor's degree, with mathematics as an optional subject. We established the Information Technology Laboratory with two dozen computers connected to a server in a local area network that also provided internet connections. All of the offices were also provided with a computer connected to the server. Faculty members were recruited to teach the courses defined for the program. Similarly, steel technology laboratories were established, and faculty members were recruited.

I commuted to Puri from Bhubaneswar every day to attend the institute. Later on, I stayed at a rented apartment in Puri. The building on the seashore was supposed to be a temporary one, and a final campus was to be established at a place near the town. A plot of about twenty acres was purchased for this purpose. However, it got mired in several controversies regarding permission from the environment ministry and encroachment issues of adjacent properties. I left BPNSI in March 2003, a little more than a year after joining.

I remember a few of the colleagues who worked with me at BPNSI: Durgesh Panda, Pradeep Mahalik, Pravat Sahu, and many others. We trained a batch of students in IT and steel technology in the building overlooking the great Bay of Bengal in the holiest temple town of Odisha. That, in itself, was a rejuvenating experience in my efforts to help Odisha and India! By this time, I had already worked at a private educational institute, and now at an institute supported by the state and the central government. I knew now how they worked and were managed, and did not have any more desire to have that kind of experience. I had to focus now on PanNet and put all my efforts there!

14. A Miraculous Escape

It was June twentieth, 2002. It was a Sunday, and I had a leisurely morning with work in the garden, then breakfast and lunch at home. My father-in-law had come from Kolkata to visit Odisha and take care of some of his affairs in the state, especially relating to his charitable trusts, and meet the relatives in his village in Ganjam and also in Puri and Bhubaneswar. That particular Sunday, he was staying with us at our residence cum office in IRC Village, Bhubaneswar. He was supposed to catch the train to Kolkata in the evening from Bhubaneswar railway station. He had a reserved ticket for the Kanya Kumari to Howrah train, coming around 8 pm to Bhubaneswar. Usually, my driver would take him in our car to the railway station and ensure that he was put on the train. Unfortunately, our car with the driver had gone that day to Sambalpur in Western Odisha. So, we had to hire a three-wheeler and send him along with our peon to help him board the train. I just felt that I should also accompany him to the railway station to ensure his safe journey on the train. He was ninety years old but was still able to travel by train.

We started around 7 pm from our home in Nayapally, Bhubaneswar, and reached the Bhubaneswar railway station, about 5km away. We came to learn that the train was late by at least half an hour. The train was supposed to come on the main platform #1 of the station. It was lightly raining at the station. After a short while, there was an announcement from the loudspeakers that the particular train would arrive at platform #3 instead of platform#1. We had to rush to the overbridge and move the belongings to the other side. Our peon, Santosh, and I carried the stuff and walked upstairs on the overbridge and then down the stairs to platform #3. We waited there for the train to arrive.

The rains continued. After some time, the electric power at the platform went off. There was the announcement that the train was arriving at the platform very soon. We anxiously waited at the platform, carrying all the bags. The train was already a couple of hours late and was going to stop at Bhubaneswar for only five minutes to allow passengers to disembark and board. We had to find the proper sleeper reserved coach and then carry the things inside the coach to the proper seat number. We had to keep the things around the reserved seat and let him sit at his seat, and then leave. By the time I kept the stuff I was carrying, the train had started to move. So, I rushed toward the door to get down.

It was raining outside, and still very dark since there was no electricity. The train was moving forward at some speed that I could not ascertain. I was just concerned about getting down so that I did not miss the station and went to the next halting station, which was Cuttack, the old capital of Odisha, 25 km away. I was still relatively new to the complications of the train journey after coming back to India. I had gone a couple of times by train to and from Kolkata. I had seen people getting down from the train as it was slowly moving, and I was confident that I could do the same. There was no inkling in my mind at the time about the dangers of getting down from a moving train. I did not realize that it was already going very fast, since there was no light. I imagined that if I ran along the platform in the direction of the moving train, I would get down on the platform as I kept running in the same direction! So,

I just put my left foot on the platform to start running on the platform. Next, I realized that I had fallen below the platform between the railway track and the platform walls. The train was moving fast above. My first thought was that I got lucky and escaped being cut into pieces, and that if something did not hit me as the train was moving, I would be OK!

Suddenly, the train stopped. So, I got up on the platform and sat on the bench on the platform. I realized now that my left foot was bleeding. A person who was sitting in the next coach saw me falling below the platform. He pulled the emergency brake of the train, and the train stopped. He was a journalist coming from Berhampur in Odisha, a distance of 180 km from Bhubaneswar, and was going beyond Bhubaneswar. He curtailed his journey and came to the bench as I sat drawn. As I put my left foot down on the platform, I was dragged, and the shoe came off, and I fell on my back on the platform. I was then sucked down onto the side of the speeding train. I must have fallen below the platform just before another coach, since I did not collide with the train as I fell.

I learned later that Santosh, who was with me carrying things into the reserved sleeper coach, jumped down a few moments after me, running away from the train. He fell on the platform and hurt his head. He did not see me around and hence went home and told Anuradha that he did not know where I was.

After I sat down on the platform bench, I felt relief that I had come out in one piece, and was top of the platform. There was no pain in the feet, but it was bleeding. I felt that it was urgent to get into a hospital as soon as possible to an emergency ward so that they could stop the bleeding. I had never gone to a hospital in Bhubaneswar. We had once admitted Anuradha into a private CARE hospital, which was now closed for good due to some personnel problems. I knew that the government Hospital #6 was not too far away, and hence both of us got into an autorickshaw and went to Hospital#6, which was just a few km away from the railway station.

We arrived at the emergency ward of Hospital#6. They roughly wrapped my left foot with some bandage cloth to stop the bleeding. I was then put on the floor there, in the emergency room. I then called my friend and high schoolmate, Ganga Rath, and told him that I was lying on the floor in the emergency room of Hospital#6. We decided that I should move immediately to Kalinga Hospital to perform the proper emergency care needed. Kalinga Hospital was started a few years back with the financing and active support of a group of Odia doctors in the United States. The Government of Odisha had provided the land needed for the hospital and the research units.

I was taken to the emergency ward of the Kalinga Hospital after my friend Ganga Rath came. Anuradha also came there, and I was admitted to the hospital and taken to a private room. An initial checkup by the doctors showed that four of the fingers in my left foot had to be amputated. There was no question of reattaching the part of the skin and other stuff that had come out since the staff at Hospital #6 had already thrown those away and had roughly bandaged the foot. Amputation would make sure that there would not be any complications during the healing process. So, I was scheduled to go through this operation the next morning.

I went through the amputation operation the next morning. Dr. Baliarsingh also scraped a bit of my skin from the side of my left leg to attach to the foot area where the skin had come off. A few days after that operation, I felt a swelling bump on my back, on the right side, where I, perhaps, landed on the ground while falling on the platform. So, another doctor extracted that mass of fluid. I was in the Kalinga hospital for two weeks, completely in bed rest.

I rejoined work at Biju Patnaik National Steel Institute after two weeks, still wearing a bandage on my left foot. It took another two weeks to completely heal, and I got used to the amputated fingers in my foot.

There has not been any complication or difficulty because of the above impairment of my left foot. I thank the stars for that!

15. Life During Work Years in India

In this chapter, I will describe our social and cultural life since the year beginning in January 1998. That is when I was back in India after selling my house in Westborough, Massachusetts. Anuradha had moved to India a couple of months earlier. So, the whole family had completed its move and had our belongings back at the IRC Village house.

Living at IRC Village

Arun was now used to his college and home life in India. We wanted to perform the thread ceremony for Arun, now that he was seventeen, and his grandparents were getting old. He was also keen to go through that. We decided to have that in early March. One February, late evening, I got a telephone call from Canada, and Dr. Radhakrishna Padhi was frantically trying to talk with me, but the line was not very clear, and we ended the call soon. A few days later, we heard from his family that he had died, apparently from a heart attack, when no one was at home. His wife had gone on a trip with her schoolmates for a trip to the Caribbean. His younger son, Devkumar, was staying close by in Vancouver and had spoken to him a few days earlier. The body was discovered when our aunt came back from vacation. That was a tragic end to the life of the heart surgeon! My father-in-law, who was about fifteen years older than his brother, performed the Shraddha kriya for his brother in Puri, since he was sure that nothing like that would have taken place in Canada for him. We moved the thread ceremony by a couple of weeks.

The ceremonies on the day before 'Bratopayana' were held inside the house and on the cemented 'vedi' in the lawn of the house. The actual thread ceremony was held at Devasthanam Mandapam in Nayapally, Bhubaneswar. We had the ground floor for food and the upstairs for ceremonies and interaction among the guests. We had also arranged a stage outside where we had dance and sangeet before the dinner. We had invited all of our relatives and friends. It was a good gathering of about four hundred persons, and we fed them an excellent vegetarian dinner.

Having the company right next to the residence made it easier for us to manage the house and the company at the same time, especially for Anuradha, but it also introduced other complexities. Sometimes, the engineering work would go to midnight or later, and we had to be just cognizant of that from the security and privacy perspectives. One special advantage during the first two years was that it allowed Arun to get involved in the company activities, especially in the development of the multimedia products. He wrote some of the sections for the CD, 'The Land of Black Krishna'. He also had the opportunity to be tutored in mathematics by Himansu, one of the software engineers working at the company. Arun told me that that was the best tutoring in mathematics he ever had, and he breezed through all his tests in the BJB College in Bhubaneswar and later in America. He had lost interest in mathematics during his middle school years in America for some unknown reason. I had a mathematics tutoring company in Framingham teach him for a year during his eighth grade, and later, one of the mathematics teachers from his high school in Westborough came to our house a couple of times every week to teach him. I had taught him during his primary school years and earlier, but we did not have time to teach then, and did not want to press him to do well. We wanted someone else to help him get back his interest in mathematics. Anyway, it certainly helped Arun to have gone through the mathematics classes in Bhubaneswar during his pre-university years in India. He did fine in his other optional subjects, logic, sociology, and psychology. He did fine also in his compulsory subjects, English, Alternate English, and general studies. He established a good rapport with his psychology lecturers at the BJB College and was also interested in the counseling of the specially handicapped children. Overall, they were two fruitful years for Arun in India. He got exposed to psychology and the psychologists in more detail and chose to apply for a degree in psychology at universities in the United States.

The two years in India were also a deep learning experience for Arun from the cultural and sociological perspectives. He went through the thread ceremony in March 1998 and attended many of the functions held at our ancestral village, Berhampur, Puri, and Bhubaneswar. He also had the opportunity to accompany me on a car trip that I took to Balangir as part of the marketing activity to sell college management software products. We stayed at my eldest brother's house in Balangir, and he saw this part of the family.

I had arranged for Arun to learn Odissi singing in Bhubaneswar, and he routinely had these lessons at our house from the well-known singer Ghanashyam Panda. He also continued his tennis lessons. He had bought a two-wheeler for himself for all of his transportation, rather than being chauffeured in a car, and had established a good set of friends from the college and outside.

Supporting Arun for Education in America

When the time came in the fall of 1998 to apply for admission to the colleges in the United States, he applied for admission to Harvard University in Cambridge, MA, Brown University in Providence, RI, Columbia University in New York City, and the University of Illinois, Urbana-Champaign. The first three of the colleges were the well-known ones in the Northeast of the United States, and the last one was my alma mater in the Midwest of the United States. He had applied everywhere for admission into the psychology programs. We did not hear from any of the colleges in spring 1999, and were very concerned that he did not apply to more universities. I was in the United States at the time, and I contacted the admissions office at Brown. Some of his classmates in Westborough were being accepted at Brown. I did not get any positive signal. I wrote to the University of Illinois as an alumnus regarding the admission of my son, stating his special and unique qualifications. Arun, finally, received a letter from the University of Illinois giving him admission to the psychology program. I was happy that he was going to my old university and that it would be good for him compared to any of those Ivy League universities that he aspired to. I also liked the fact that he was going to be on a campus far from any big city and would be relatively safe there.

Anuradha taught him how to prepare a few Indian dishes so that he could prepare them when he had to. After flying to the United States, we drove together in our car to Urbana-Champaign from Massachusetts. We stayed in a hotel there and then dropped him off at the allotted hall of residence. Arun had already met some of the residents of the hostel on the first day and had made friends, but was teary-eyed, since this was the first time he was being left alone, and we would be far off in India.

Arun adjusted to his campus life and was doing fine in his classes. On October 22nd, 1999, came the super-cyclone in Odisha, and it was reported in the American news that Bhubaneswar was off the map and almost wiped out. For many days, there was no communication with us. Fortunately, we did not have too many problems at our IRC Village residence. There was no electricity, and fortunately, there was water in our overhead tank. No trees were blown away near our house. There was, however, water on the floor of all the rooms in the living quarters and the company premises, because water seeped through all the gaps in the windows and doors due to the extremely high wind of 300km. Many of our carpets and drapes were damaged. The company was closed for a week until the power and water were restored. Arun was able to contact my sister-in-law in Kolkata after a few days and learnt that everything was fine. During the Christmas vacation, he visited with the family of some of his college friends. He visited India during the summer vacation and was happy to be back at home.

The following summer in the year 2001, I was in the Fall River townhouse. So, Arun flew to Massachusetts after his classes were over in June. I taught him how to drive, and he obtained a driving license in Massachusetts. I bought a secondhand Toyota Corolla for myself to be kept at Fall River, and wanted to give Arun the old Toyota Camry so that he could use it on the campus. We drove the car together to Urbana-Champaign from Fall River, and I left the car with him, and then flew back to Massachusetts.

Arun visited India during the Christmas vacation of 2001. We visited Chennai and Tirupati and then took the train back to Bhubaneswar. During the summer of 2002, Arun stayed on the campus and attended summer courses, and then worked at a restaurant on the campus as a waiter. That was the only time that he had worked, and it was a good experience for him, as he described. I had my train accident that summer in June 2002, and after I had recovered, I flew to Boston in October 2002 and sold the last of my townhouses in Fall River. I kept the belongings in a storage at Fall River so that some of the things could be used by Arun or us, depending on the situation. I drove to the campus in Urbana-Champaign and gave the car to Arun for his use. He had already given the earlier car to a friend.

Arun graduated from the University of Illinois in June 2003 with a Bachelor of Science degree in Psychology. Unfortunately, we could not attend his graduation ceremony, and he missed us, since all of his friends had their parents attend the ceremony. He visited India that summer and had the time to renew the relationship with all the relatives in Bhubaneswar, Puri, Berhampur, and Kolkata. He had applied for admission into the medical school in the USA and secured admission into the University of Massachusetts Medical School at Worcester. We were very happy that he had been successful in getting through the tough selection processes and was going to study in Worcester, which was only about ten miles away from our earlier residence in Westborough. I arranged for him to live with one of his classmates in the incoming class in the medical college, Bharat, who owned this two-bedroom apartment overlooking the lake Quinsigamond. He stayed there along with Bharat for the four years of his stay in the medical school at the University of Massachusetts. Arun went to Fall River and got a few of our dining and other furniture from the storage. I donated the rest of the belongings in the storage to charity after a few months. I would visit every year and stay with Arun for a week or more, there in Worcester. Arun also visited India during the summer vacations and the December breaks.

Once Arun was in medical school, we started looking for a bride for him, especially after the completion of the first year, when he had come to India for the summer break. My father-in-law was sick then and was being taken care of at his apartment on Gariahat Road in south Kolkata. He expired in July 2004 at the age of ninety-two, when Arun happened to be in Kolkata. I was in Kolkata at the time on a marketing mission along with PanNet Marketing Manager of Kolkata, Nirmalya Sinha. We waited for Anuradha to arrive from Bhubaneswar, and then took the body to the cremation hall. All of the Shraddha ceremonies and feasts were held in Ballygunge in the apartment building. Arun led the religious ceremonies as the grandson.

The following year, January 2005, I started looking for a candidate by putting his profile on the matrimonial site Shaadi.com. There were several candidates, and we chose one for further interaction. Arun came to India for Christmas vacation in December 2005 and met the candidate and her family. He liked the candidate, and we held a quick engagement ceremony before Arun left for America. His fiancée went to the United States in the fall of 2006 to do a Master's degree in Health Administration. Now, there was more scope for interaction in America, but soon they found themselves to be unsuitable for each other, and hence this engagement was cancelled by mutual agreement. The main problem of incompatibility was the fact that Arun did not want his fiancée to be controlled by her parents and expected to be a couple free from control by parents from both sides. Girls raised in India are usually not that independent in their behavior and in carrying out responsibilities. We were more patient and careful now and wanted to focus on candidates raised in the United States.

House at VIP Colony

I had been slowly planning a transition from the business world to the eventual world of retirement without any business interests. When I became sixty years old in 2005, I decided at that time that I had to make a full transition to retirement life by the year 2010, when I would be sixty-five. So, there was a five-year period by which I would have achieved, to the best of my capabilities, whatever remaining aims I had regarding business, wealth creation, and building a retirement home.

It was clear to me that I did not want to live in the house at N3-B6, IRC Village, Nayapally, Bhubaneswar, where I had my company on the side building. It was at the crossing of two main roads and relatively busy and noisy, especially in front of the main building side with the two-lane road. Although the other side of the building, where there was the entrance for the company, had a divided four-lane road, any street noise was shielded due to the side garden that was developed and maintained by us. This garden was the most attractive part of this property, and we maintained our residence next to the company premises for that reason. But I was sure that I wanted to live in retirement in front of the largest garden in Bhubaneswar. For a period of five years from 1997 to 2001, I did not do any more construction on my property at VIP Colony Plot -7, and the ground floor rooms were used to give free shelter to some carpenters living alone and others, especially during and after the great cyclone of October 1999, which devastated coastal Odisha.

I employed a local architect to re-examine the original blueprint of the building and the partially completed building. Some of our requirements had changed as we better understood the climatic conditions in Bhubaneswar. The architect suggested alterations and additions for the second and third floors. We restarted construction in the year 2002. Enhancements were planned to make the home an attractive one:

1. The bedroom behind the master bedroom was combined with the latter to make a grand-size room with a Jacuzzi and a wraparound balcony in the front and the back.
2. The entry porch and the balcony on its top were covered with a sloping roof supported by four circular and decorated columns to project a grand view from the front.
3. A portico in front of the garage was constructed with the support of four matching one-foot circular decorated columns.
4. A triangular protrusion supported by four decorative columns, similar to what is in the front part of the Whitehouse in Washington, was added to cover the two main front windows of the master bedroom.
5. The so-called guest room on the southeast corner of the building was made wider by about three feet by adding a beam supported by two square column structures.
6. The third-floor roof was redesigned to include a square glass structure to project light to the stairs area.
7. The cutout of the floor above the dining room was

decreased in size and made into a curvy decorative inside balcony.
8. The second-floor room adjoining the outside stairs to the third floor was designed to have tall glass windows at the front and back.
9. A bathroom was added to the second floor on top of the stairs below.
10. The second-floor front room was designed to have a slanted roof with a triangular front view, and a massive glass door ten feet wide was planned in the front of the room, providing access to the open circular balcony at the front of the house.

With all these alterations and additions, the building at VIP Colony provided the following facilities:

Ground Floor consisted of Entry porch, Entry foyer, Library room with adjoining bathroom, kitchen, garage room, and open portico behind the garage and on the side of the house.

The first floor consisted of the master bedroom with powder room and bathroom, guest bedroom with bath, two bedrooms on the side sharing a bathroom, a covered balcony and adjoining sitting area inside, and an open work and entertainment corner on top of the dining room.

The second floor consisted of the large front room with the front glass door and window, and a smaller office cum bedroom sharing a bathroom with two separate doors. The terrace on this floor could have a garden. The third-floor terrace had access from the open stairs from the second floor.

The building at VIP Colony was finally completed at the end of 2005, and we moved there from our IRC Village building in November 2006. So, finally, I had a home that would be the last one where I could spend the rest of my life!

Engagement and Marriage of Arun

Arun completed his medical degree from the University of Massachusetts in May 2007, and I attended his graduation ceremony in Worcester. He had applied for residency in pediatrics and was admitted into the program at Tufts University in Boston. So, we got him a studio apartment in Boston on rent, and transferred all his belongings from Worcester to Boston.

In the fall of 2007, I had asked Arun to meet a candidate who was working in Boston. They met, and both of them seemed to like each other. I visited Boston in the spring of 2008 and met Swapna Punchagnula and her parents, Dr. Shastri Punchagnula and Jyothika Punchagnula, from Ohio. Anuradha later went along with Arun to visit Swapna's parents' house on the outskirts of Cleveland. Swapna and Arun then took a trip to Morocco, where Arun proposed to her, and they were engaged to be married. Before marriage, they wanted to stay together for a year in Boston. So, they got a two-bedroom apartment right on top of the Italian market section of Boston, where there were the best Italian restaurants. Arun continued his residency at Tufts, and Swapna kept on working as an accountant at one of the CPA firms in Boston. Swapna and Arun were married after about a year in Cleveland on August 30, 2009. Arun and Swapna planned this marriage and arranged it in a hotel in Cleveland. I came to the United States first, and then Anuradha came along with her mother to attend the wedding. There was a day of sangeet and entertainment before the wedding day. The wedding was performed in the Hindu tradition in front of an altar of fire, fed by Indian purified butter. There was a gala dinner and entertainment in the evening. Many of our friends from Massachusetts were there: Satyabrata and Dola Mishra, Amaresh and

Sadhna Mahapatra, and a few of Arun's friends. My friend Omprakash Agrawal and his wife Hema Agrawal had come from California to attend the marriage.

We all flew back to Bhubaneswar for a reception at the hotel Mayfair in Nayapally on September 6th. We had decorated our VIP Colony house, especially the second-floor terrace, where a sangeet ceremony was held in the evening before the day of the reception for all friends and relatives. At the dinner reception in Mayfair, we had entertainment, special songs in Hindi and Odia, accompanied by a band. All of our relatives and friends had come from all over Odisha and Kolkata to take part in the reception. On the day after the reception, Arun and Swapna left for their honeymoon in Fiji in the Pacific.

We were happy that we had completed one of our major parental responsibilities by shuffling between India and America. It was not all the way smooth, but luckily got done on time. Anuradha had to take a big burden of informing all our relatives and friends in Berhampur, Balangir, Puri, and Bhubaneswar by going to everyone's house and giving the invitation for the reception ceremony at Bhubaneswar. Then she had to fly to America with her mother for the marriage ceremony in Cleveland.

The year after Arun's marriage was spent preparing for eventual retirement from the business operations. As reported earlier, PanNet had to go through a set of restructuring steps to align the manpower and the facilities with the changing business conditions. We closed the operation of PanNet in the year 2010. It took quite a bit of time that year to just clear up the company facilities at the IRC Village house. We gave away some office furniture to a private health support group in Bhubaneswar. We kept a limited set of office furniture and equipment in the two ground-floor rooms that we planned to keep as our private office for the charitable activities during our retirement years. I was now sixty-five years old, and it was time for retirement from business activities!

Part IV
Retirement World in India
(2010 to 2025)

16. World of Social Work and Charity
17. Zen, Advaita, and Writing
18. World of Business Mentorship
19. Revisiting My Different Worlds
20. The Road to Nirvana!

16. World of Social Work and Charity

When I was sixty-five years old in the year 2010, I did not want to be engaged in any business ventures for profit, except for passive investments in real estate and passive stock investments. But I was physically and mentally in good shape to be active in social work and charitable activities.

I explored the possibility of working with educational institutions for any research opportunities and visited IIT Bhubaneswar and other organizations. All of them were essentially engaged in teaching and not research. Neither did I want to fund a private technical research foundation, nor did I have the funds to do that. So, I decided to devote my time to social work activities and possibly do some writing. In this chapter, I describe some of the charitable activities.

Purushottam Trust

My father-in-law had donated 50% of the investment in his stock portfolio to two charitable trusts. These were consolidated into one of the trusts, Purushottam Trust. Sometime after my father-in-law's death in July 2004, we spent considerable time straightening out all the bank accounts and trust documents. A new board of directors was constituted with Anuradha as Managing Director and with me as one of the directors. The other directors were Anuradha's mother, younger sister Sushama, and her husband Pratap Pathy.

Purushottam Trust has been operating more in a dormant mode since the demise of my father-in-law, mainly since the income generated from the trust funds had declined considerably in terms of interest and dividends. Earlier considerable amount of funds was spent on building and maintaining the temple in Khajuria and then supporting the college in Chikiti. The funds from the trust were donated to various organizations in small amounts, as and when needed. Some of the organizations that received donations from the trust were the following: Rotary Clubs of Bhubaneswar, Bhubaneswar Music Circle, Kripalu Maharaj, and many specific individuals in need.

Since Purushottam Trust had made big contributions to constructing the Radhakrishna temple in the village of Khajuria, one of our responsibilities was to ensure that the temple managed its affairs and maintained the property. We are happy to note that the temple has managed all its affairs without any support from the Purushottam trust for more than a decade now.

A substantial portion of the money from the trust was used ten years ago to buy a piece of land of about three thousand square feet near the second IT city (Info Valley) coming up on the outskirts of Bhubaneswar. We intend to build here a spiritual and arts center that could be utilized for the benefit of society, especially for educating the underprivileged and talented children and youth in the coming years. We need to make substantial personal contributions in the coming years, both in terms of time and further financial resources, to make this happen.

SriHari Trust

I had registered SriHari Trust in the name of my late father, Hari Panigrahi, to operate a charitable organization in our village, Bodoboranga. The other members of the trust were my two nephews and their wives. In addition, my schoolmate in the village school, Lopinti Jogulu, was also made a director of the trust. My goal was to donate to the trust the value of whatever I had owned in the village at the time, and additional funds to construct a village club-like institute for the use of the villagers.

I planned for a library room, an exercise room with an attached bathroom, plus a large and wide front room in front of those two rooms, which can be used for classes, meetings, and other activities. This front room would have wide front doors so that the room could be used as a stage for performances. This would be like a mini version of the Hatch Shell that I had seen by the side of the Charles River in Boston. There would be some open area in front of the building for people to sit and watch the performances. The whole ground floor would be covered with a flat cement roof, and the stairs to be built at the back of the building to go up to the terrace. Thus, the terrace could be used for big feasts or other celebrations.

I negotiated with my younger nephew, Sudama, to get a plot right next to his shop that stored construction products on the side of the main road at the entrance of the village. The building was finally constructed over a period of three years with the help of my elder nephew, Sudarshan, who arranged and supervised things as per my building plan. The building was finally completed in 2015, and we inaugurated it.

My initial vision was that this building should be used for the female folks of the village as their exclusive club.

The Shiva temple and the mutt at the ends of the village were mostly used by the males for activities, except during the religious celebrations, when everyone visited these places. There was no place in the village for the women to congregate and work together. In the old days, the ghats in the river worked as the gossip and social venues for the women, and they were gone now. So, I called this building 'Naaree Mahal' and invited men, women, and children to participate in the opening day. I visited many families in the village to personally invite the women to participate. We had an opening day with about a hundred people participating. Sweets and fruits were distributed along with soft drinks.

I demonstrated to them how the facilities could be used for recreational activities, and possibly, for commercial purposes too. The library was provided with a large number of different books, and we could get newspapers and other facilities as they started using it. The health room was provided with stationary cycles and a rowing machine for exercise. One could perform yoga in the Health Room or the front Common Room.

We enlisted a few of the ladies, including the daughter of my cousin, to take leadership and start using the facility. Strangely enough, there was not much leadership coming from the women because there was no history of a female-only club or organization, and they were always led by the male members in the village. So, after waiting for about two years, I decided that we have to make it a general educational, recreational, vocational, and health institution for all members of the village. I went to the village and had a special meeting with the male leaders who were interested in transforming it into a health club for the young and the old. A sum of one lakh was used to buy special equipment for trade-mill exercises and more stationary bikes.

Hopefully, the residents of Bodoboranga will use this facility more as a cultural center with daily and weekly activities for societal growth and development. One recent suggestion they are exploring to start is to have a weekly Sunday program where children and adults can listen to dharmic recitations and discussion.

Ekamrakhetra Rotary

With the help of my schoolmate and friend Girish Mohanty, we started a new Rotary club that started operating in the year 2013-2014 and had members from the surrounding area. We met almost weekly either in our facility at N3-B6, IRC Village, or at another bigger facility, Fakir Mohan Bhavan in the VIP Colony.

The club regularly visited Chunakoli, a village on the outskirts of Bhubaneswar, where tribals from different parts of eastern India had settled down. The primary school in the village did not have adequate facilities, and the club members cleaned the outside premises of the school and planted many trees. During the Independence Day and Republic Day celebrations, we often went there to distribute sweets to the students of the school. Another charitable organization had constructed a building adjacent to the primary school, which was being used as a clubhouse by the members of the village, especially the females of the village. We participated in many meetings where we offered special programs for the women and men of the village: health check-ups and medicine distributions, adult literacy instructions, and special skills development. One such program for the women was to manufacture bundles of incense sticks and package them into well-designed and branded paper boxes.

A special grant from the government administration was obtained for this purpose, and a bank account was opened to purchase the materials required. The incense boxes were sold to the public at exhibitions and to rotary members at the club meetings.

The adult literacy program was started at Chunakoli village with the assistance of the mass education organization of the Government of Odisha. Instructions were given a couple of times during the week. The success of the program was uneven, and many of the women did not want to continue with the program since they did not see any monetary benefits from their labor at that particular stage of their lives.

After the experience at Chunakoli for a few years, the rotary group adopted a village near the Mancheswar industrial estate to enable the girls and women of the village to learn the stitching of sweaters and the tailoring of dresses. Half a dozen sewing machines were provided, and trainers were invited to train. Most of these girls learned the craft, and it was a success in that way. But the group slowly melted away as the girls got married and moved away from the locality. We had to restart to form a new group of women who would be interested in this business from that locality, or else try to relocate the sewing machines to another needy area around Bhubaneswar.

Both Anuradha and I have continued our participation in the rotary club activities to keep us engaged with the communities around Bhubaneswar.

Sunday Morning Free School

A children's Sunday free school was opened at our IRC Village house in April 2016 to help students from the surrounding areas who came from disadvantaged communities. The students were divided into two groups: the lower group studying in grades III to VI and the higher group studying grades VII to X. They were given instructions in three primary subjects: Mathematics, English, and the sciences. In addition, they were exposed to topics in social studies. The school was conducted mainly every week on Sunday mornings. Additional classes were planned for the students in the higher grades as the need arose.

This school operated for a couple of years and was mainly taught by Anuradha. I used to take some of the classes in mathematics and the sciences. It was stopped in the summer of the year 2018 when Anuradha got too busy with the care of her mother, who lived with us and was ailing, and I was away in the United States for quite some time. The students in the group also graduated from the high schools passing out the tenth grade that year. We did not start with a new group after that.

Free School for Slum Children

A school for the slum children in the Mancheshwar Industrial area has been maintained since the year 2016. These children and young adults are from a community that had moved from Uttar Pradesh to the Bhubaneswar area almost forty to fifty years back, but had not enlisted in the local schools or taken advantage of water, electricity, and other advantages of the municipal government. We helped them get the registration of the individuals and then guided the children to eventually admit them to the local schools. Many of the young adults also participated in the slum school to learn reading and writing. The adults of this community mainly worked as hawkers in the surrounding areas in the afternoon and evening. Hence, a morning school for a couple of hours was beneficial to them without impacting earnings from their livelihood.

This school has been operating for many years, especially because of the efforts by Anuradha and the teacher who has been teaching and helping the children of the slum school every day for a couple of hours.

17. Zen, Advaita and Writing

In this chapter, I describe how I traversed through the spiritual world during my retirement years and got exposed to Mahayana Buddhism, and later joined Zen Buddhist retreats and started the Zen sangha in Bhubaneswar. These steps led me to the writing projects that have become the backbone of my retirement years.

Mahayana Buddhism

In December 1968, during my first Christmas vacation in the United States of America, I picked up a book, 'Outlines of Mahayana Buddhism', at the Illini Union Bookstore. I glanced through the pages of this book written by D. T. Suzuki, but I never had the time to fully go through the book and understand all the ramifications of Mahayana Buddhism. Many years later, when I was residing in Westborough, Massachusetts, I had the urge to go through some of the pages of the book again as I was exploring more about Buddhism. I attended one or two meetings of the Buddhist group of Vajrayana following in the Newton area. I wanted to attend the Zen group meetings in Providence, Rhode Island, which were being conducted by the Korean priest. I also signed up a few times to attend the Vipassana retreats in Amherst, Massachusetts, but could not make it to the retreats.

After coming back to India, I was too busy during the first fifteen years to devote any time to religious pursuits. After I closed PanNet Computer, I had more time to explore religion in the Bhubaneswar area. I attended a few early morning meetings held at the headquarters of Chinmay Mission, which was just a few blocks behind my residence in the VIP Colony. I also attended a few of the lectures on the Gita, delivered by the head of Chinmay Mission at the DAV School, Chandrasekharpur, Bhubaneswar. I often had discussions with one of my elderly neighbors about various religions, and it became apparent to me at the time that there was hardly any knowledge of Mahayana Buddhism in Odisha. There were no books in Odia or any other Language on Mahayana Buddhism in the premier library in Bhubaneswar. I could not locate any books on Mahayana Buddhism at the National Library situated in Kolkata. That is when I decided to translate the book 'Outlines of Mahayana Buddhism' by D.T. Suzuki.

That was a daring undertaking at the time since I had hardly done much reading or writing in Odia for almost fifty years. But I had the confidence that I could retrieve my capabilities since I was very active in writing in high school and was the literary editor of the school in my tenth class. I was also convinced that this would allow me to have a deeper understanding of the various facts of Mahayana Buddhism.

I started translating it, beginning year 2011, and went on from chapter after chapter from the beginning, except for the preparatory essay by Alan Watts, the Buddhist philosopher and professor. I had almost completed the translations near the end of the year 2012. At that time, I had gone to the Buddha temple at Bhubaneswar and met Dr. Bimalendu Mohanty, President of the Buddhist organization. He happened to live not far from my residence. I was able to use his typist to get the transcripts into the typed version. I went through the typed pages painstakingly to correct any errors. A final version was prepared early in the year 2013 and then published with the help of Dr. Sourendra K. Mahapatra, the secretary of the Buddhist organization, who also designed the front and back covers of the book. Five hundred copies of the book were printed. Thus started my journey to the world of religion and philosophy. This was my first big step. I also became a confident writer and realized the enjoyment of the writing process, lonely and secluded from other activities. I set up my writing and research desks in the room at the center of the second floor of my house in the VIP Colony. This allowed me to peek at my terrace garden and the tall trees standing in front of the vast Ekamrakanan Park while being isolated from the goings on underneath.

Kalinga ZEN Advaita Mahasangha

In the spring of the year 2014, I had the opportunity to attend the seven-day Zen retreat in southern New Jersey arranged by Roshi Kankan (Professor Kurt Spellmeyer of Rutgers University). I was very eager and planned to attend it since the Fall of 2013, and yet was very apprehensive because I had never attended any meditation retreat. We had to get up at 4.30 AM every morning and be engaged in about ten hours of meditation every day, intertwined with morning garden work, meal-time, clean-up, afternoon siesta, garden work, and walking meditation. Fortunately, I was able to bear through all the rigors of the retreat, and on the last full day of the retreat, I found sweat running through my face and body, a sense of heaviness on my forehead, and a reluctance to get up from the blissful state. I had the experience of so-called 'emptiness'.

In search of the same journey through meditation, I attended retreats once every year from 2015 to 2018 in the spring, respectively at New York Zen Mountain Monastery, Roshi Konkan's South Jersey Retreat, Tahoma Sogen-ji Zen Monastery in the state of Washington, and finally the Shasta Mountain Monastery retreat in California. These retreats exposed me to the different aspects of Zen Buddhism in the United States.

During August and September 2015, I organized a set of meetings of the members of the Mahabodhi Society of India, Bhubaneswar, to educate interested persons on Zen Buddhism and its meditation practice. I shifted this group to the ground-floor rooms in my N3-B6 building in IRC Village. This allowed the group to practice in an exclusive area with a big green park in the front. A statue of a standing Buddha was installed at the back of the cemented square platform outside. 'Kalinga ZEN Foundation Trust' was later registered in Bhubaneswar as a charitable trust to support the activities of this Zen group called 'Kalinga ZEN Advaita Mahasangha'. The adjective Advaita was used since nonduality is the main tenet of Zen Buddhism, and also because I intended to incorporate into it the same aspects of 'Advaita Vedanta', the premier Hindu sect also emphasizing nonduality.

Over the years, we have established a reference library of books on Zen, Mahayana Buddhism, Theravada, Vajrayana, Hinduism, and Indic studies, including the history and culture of Odisha. This library has been critical in performing the research activities that we embarked upon later. To support and sustain the activities of the sangha, the following books have been written by me:

1. Heart of Zen Buddhism: A Garland of Quotes, 2017
2. Zen Bauddhadharma: Darshana O Pratha, 2018 (in Odia)
3. Zen Bauddhadharmara Moolatatva, 2020 (in Odia)

4. Zen Buddhism: Doctrinal Foundations and Practice, 2021
5. Zen Buddhism and Advaita Vedanta: A Comparative Study of History, Philosophy, and Practice, 2024
6. The Buddha Reveals: His Love and Enlightenment, 2024

Advaita Dhyana Kalaasangha

The Kalinga ZEN Advaita Mahasangha completed ten years of its existence in Bhubaneswar in August 2025. During its existence, it has exposed hundreds of people to Zen and Buddhism. In its new Avatar, we are renaming it 'Advaita Dhyana Kalaasangha'. The word 'Dhyana' is replacing 'Zen', since the word Zen was the Japanese rendering of the word 'Dhyana'. The word Zen in India is always confused with Jain and Jainism, especially in the spoken form. We are using the word 'Kalaasangha' instead of 'Mahasangha', since one of the main goals of the rejuvenated new organization is to integrate the fine arts, especially singing, dance, and culture, into the sangha activities.

One project started in 2025 is 'Jnanodaya Abhijan', where our goal is to teach young children, aged ten and higher, about Indian culture, languages, and sangeet in a Sunday morning school at as many places, starting in Bhubaneswar. This should fill a gap in the present Indian society, where the young people are only taught about career skills and scoring in examinations, and these other life goals and behaviors are neglected by their parents. As a first step, we are starting a ten-month program to teach the following three classes, beginning August 17th, 2025:
1. 9.00 AM to 9.40 AM: Culture
   Indian Dharmas, Traditions, Yoga, and Dhyana
   Odia Language and Literature

2. 9.40 AM to 10.20 AM: Spoken Sanskrit and Slokas
   Conversational Sanskrit
   Dharma Slokas from Hinduism, Buddhism, and Jainism
3. 10.20 AM to 11.00 AM: Sangeet
   Bhajan and Patriotic Songs in Odia and Hindi
   Hindustani Music

Advaita Dhyana Kalaasangha appointed three qualified college teachers who conducted these classes. These are multi-year programs that could be imparted up to two levels of proficiency. The first batch of students started on 17th August 2025. They are all girls from the Salia Sahi area studying in 8th to 10th grade at Indradhanu Market Government High School. Hopefully, this pioneering batch can guide us as to how this program can be extended to more places. A few of the elders, including myself, have also enrolled in these classes. It is never too late to sharpen one's Sanskrit and learn to sing!

Research on Dharmic Religions

We had contemplated that Kalinga ZEN Advaita Mahasangha would impart college-level teaching on Zen and Buddhism to aspiring students and award them degrees under the auspices of Utkal University of Culture (UCC). However, this plan did not succeed due to the denial of permission by the UCC and the Department of Culture of the Government of Odisha, despite several interactions during the years 2020 to 2022. So, we decided to focus our future efforts on research. In that context, we started a project in November 2022 to compare and contrast Zen Buddhism and Advaita Vedanta. Debi Prasad Dash, who had just completed a Master of Arts degree in philosophy, was hired as a full-time Research Assistant to work with me on this project. He was given an appointment for a period of one year by the Kalinga ZEN Foundation. Brigadier Niranjan Dhal, a key member of the sangha, also supported financially in this research venture.

We worked every day in the sangha meditation room in a solitary environment, having all the discussions and writings while sitting on a Zen Zafu. The result of the effort was the publication of the book, 'Zen Buddhism and Advaita Vedanta: A Comparative Study of History, Philosophy, and Practice'. The book was published by BlackEagle Books in the middle of 2024. Through its chapters on the history, metaphysics, epistemology, ethics, aesthetics, and practice, the book provided a comprehensive introduction to both Zen Buddhism and Advaita Vedanta, the two premier sects of Buddhism and Hinduism, respectively, that are non-dual.

Writing on the Buddha

As I was discovering the different aspects of Buddhism and studying the life history of the Buddha, a more humane story of the Buddha grew up inside me. I felt compelled to investigate further and visit some of the key places in the Buddha's life, and then started writing the story as if the Buddha told his story through me. So, it came out as a historical novel on the Buddha's life. This was mainly written during a period of five years between 2015 and 2019. With further revisions and additions, it was published in December 2024 by BlackEagle Books and was opened at a ceremony at the Mahabodhi Society of India, Bhubaneswar, marking the enlightenment day (Rohatsu) in the Buddha's life. The book was titled, 'The Buddha Reveals: His Love and Enlightenment'.

The above book also included seven poems as part of the story. Encouraged by friends, I have now written the life story of the Buddha in the form of a series of poems recited by the Buddha and the other main characters, especially his wife and disciple Yashodhara. I have also translated the same into Odia. I hope that parts of this would be further rendered into songs and enacted as scenes for a play on the life of the Buddha. One of the goals of Advaita Dhyana Kalaasangha is to transform some of these writings into dance dramas and songs, to be performed at the sangha functions.

When in high school, I often wondered about being a poet or a writer! I remember the famous Odia poet Radha Mohan Gadnayak's line, 'Kabi Hebaku Basana Mara' (My dream to be a poet). I was an avid reader of the Odia novels by Kanhu Charan Mohanty, Gopinath Mohanty, Fakir Mohan Senapati, Kalindi Panigrahi, and many others. I read the poems in Odia by Upendra Bhanja, Baladev Ratha, Gangadhar Meher, Godavarish Mishra, Nanda Kishore Bal, and others. Similarly, I read in Hindi, Prem Chand, Suryakant Nirula, Dinkar, etc. In English, my favorite writers were Somerset Maugham, D.H. Lawrence, Jane Austen, etc., and the English translations of writers, such as Tolstoy, Dostovsky, Camus, etc., around the world. There was a deep interest in literature of all forms in those formative years.

I did some writing in school in different forms: poems, short stories, and essays. During my professional career as an electronics engineer, I wrote about two dozen articles, review papers, etc. I had also served as one of the editors of IEEE MICRO Magazine. But all of the latent urges to write were rekindled during the retirement years when I started translating the book on Mahayana Buddhism.

Now that I have published half a dozen books in Odia and English, and there are another half a dozen books in the pipeline, I have begun to develop certain discipline as a writer. I write every day in the mornings for a couple of hours or more. Writing gives intellectual ammunition to the soul within. It clarifies ideas in the mind when you put them down on paper. You also write for others to read and use the information for their enjoyment or use in their practice.

So, writing will continue as the needs arise or there is a story to tell! No doubt, the writing projects keep me very engrossed in them until I complete them. I do think about them as I take my evening walks, and also at other times at home and outside. I mostly enjoyed writing longhand with a pen on white paper sheets, and this was a fast way of dumping my thoughts on pen and paper. Nowadays, I am used to typing straight on my computer, but for Odia compositions, I have to go through the step of writing on paper, and then make corrections, after the manuscript is typed and then reproduced on paper. I have, still now, many projects in Odia on the Buddha, especially since I would like more of Buddha's stories to be available to the public in song and drama forms!

18. World of Business Mentorship

Although I had decided not to have any more business activity for personal gain, I had not ruled out guiding and helping others from an empathetic perspective. All of these involvements randomly started from casual relationships with neighbors and service providers.

Black Star Graphite

A couple of years after the closure of PanNet Computer, an opportunity came to help a friend who was having a graphite mining, beneficiation, and distribution operation running in Hindol and Bhubaneswar in Odisha. Doreen Schnurr was a neighbor of mine, staying on the front part of the top floor of the five-story apartment building next to me. She also had a terrace garden on top of her apartment and could talk to me from her apartment or the top terrace when I was on my second or third-floor terrace gardens. Doreen was brought up in Cuttack, Odisha's old Capital, just twenty km away from Bhubaneswar. She was married to a German engineer and had two adult children living in Germany. She later lived in the Washington D.C. area for about a decade with her American husband. After her husband's death, she came back to India and lived in Bhubaneswar.

Doreen was having trouble managing the graphite operation along with her partner, a young geologist from the Hindol area. The partnership agreement under which she was managing the operation was flawed. Doreen was a pure soul who wanted to do good and was proud that she was providing a livelihood to many people in the area. But she was unaware of the legal implications and personal liability. She had invested about a crore or more of Rupees, and had no more funds to invest. But she was not getting my return on the investment from the revenues earned, and rather was being sucked into paying more and more.

We allowed Doreen to move her Bhubaneswar office to the two rooms we had kept in N3-B6 IRC Village building for free. This allowed her to save the office rental charges, but more importantly, allowed us to examine the books and the papers associated with the partnership operation. Anuradha examined the financial documents, trying to analyze and set up an appropriate accounting system. We helped her stop expenses toward mining prospecting activity.

For Doreen to have full control of the enterprise, we finally set up a company, Blackstar Graphite Pvt. Ltd., where she had control of the company, with me as the President, my wife Anuradha as a director, and another director chosen by Doreen to head the manufacturing operation. The young geologist was also invited to become a director of the company. As part of this arrangement, Doreen first transferred half of the land parcel containing the factory to the company. The lawyers ensured that the land registration was done in the name of Blackstar Graphite. We had to travel a couple of times by car to the factory in Hindol and also be the guests of the erstwhile king of Hindol at his grand but dilapidated palace for the special lunch cooked by the king and his servants. So, finally, Doreen was able to manage the company to her benefit. She contracted a young man who had some business experience in the hotel industry and was very interested in managing the factory, staying at Hindol in the factory. As a result, she got some financial rewards from the revenue after sales. This whole episode took a year or more to settle down, and thereafter, both Anuradha and I acted just as advisors to Doreen for the management of Blackstar Graphite. After a year or two of operating this way, Doreen finally sold the assets of the company to the young contractor managing the factory. The company Blackstar Graphite Pvt. Ltd. was formally closed, and I signed off the documents as the President. We never expected or got any financial rewards for our involvement in Blackstar Graphite Pvt. Ltd. We spent some funds from our own pockets to straighten out the company.

Thus ended the graphite extraction and beneficiation at Hindol. But Doreen became a close friend of ours, and we had many meals and drinks together at her beautifully designed apartment with its expansive view of Ekamrakaanan. She also came down to our residence quite often to share food and drinks. We would see her going to the big Ekamrakaanan Park early at 6.30 AM or returning around 8 AM. That was her routine until the COVID-19 outbreak in 2020. She stopped the morning walks and yoga exercises in the park. She came last to have dinner with us in December 2021, when our grandson Arjun and granddaughter Amrita were staying with us after taking a six-month break from school in Davis, California, and studying at Sai International School in Bhubaneswar. Doreen had prepared a dish for all five of us. Anuradha made an elaborate dinner with the help of Soni, our cook cum driver. We all had a good meal, and the kids also heard some stories from Doreen.

A couple of days after that dinner get-together at our residence, we came to know that Doreen had a heart attack and was hospitalized at AMRI Hospital in Bhubaneswar.

She was then recuperating, staying at her apartment. We saw her a couple of times while she was in the wheelchair, assisted by a maid in her apartment and outside on the street. She never recovered fully and had more attacks, and subsequently lost her speech and was mostly in and out of hospitals for a year. Her son and daughter had come from Germany to see her. She was finally staying at a private health center where two maids were taking care of her, and the same maids were staying at her apartment to take care of her garden.

We finally saw Doreen at this private health center just a few kilometers from our residence. Her eyes were just rolling toward us, but she did not have any indication of recognizing us, and was just lying on the bed. A few days after that, she passed away and was cremated in the Bhubaneswar crematorium. A week afterward, I attended the memorial evening that was held in her apartment, arranged by her nephew (her late brother's son), sister-in-law, and friends. We miss Doreen quite a lot! She was a connoisseur of food and drinks and was equally entertaining with her stories from all over the world, from Pakistan, the Middle East, Germany, Europe, and the United States of America.

Ashiana Lagoon Trust

We had purchased a one-bedroom apartment on the top floor of Ashiana Lagoon on the Puri beach overlooking the ocean from the balcony of the apartment. This was in the year 2012. We took possession of the same a year after that.

Anuradha wanted to do a member of alterations to the apartment so that it would become a very attractive one-bedroom apartment. We had been planning to convert the balcony next to the kitchen to be enclosed with glass panes and remove the door to the balcony. We planned to install modular kitchen cabinets and change the floor of this drawing cum dining cum kitchen room. But there were problems associated with the operation and maintenance of the whole building:

1. The lift was never operated and needed to be fixed, or a new one had to be installed.
2. The builder did not establish an association of the owners for upkeep and maintenance, and just invited a fixed sum to be given to him for lifetime maintenance.
3. The swimming pool was not finished by the builder.

So, finally, some of the owners, including Anuradha, got together and a trust was formed to manage the operation. Anuradha became the Vice President of Finance and was busy managing it for years. A new lift was procured and installed. There was damage to the boundary wall and other structures during the summer cyclone in the year 2017. New and stronger boundary walls were constructed. Anuradha finally got the swimming pool working in the year 2019 after employing the person who first got our swimming pool completed at the VIP Colony residence. With the swimming pool operating at Ashiana Lagoon, it became an attractive location, and a good hotel operator was brought in to operate and maintain the building. About twenty-five of the forty owners gave their apartments for the hotel operation. That made the maintenance less costly and easier for the owners. Finally, we had the time to make all the changes in our one-bedroom apartment and were able to stay the first night there in the year 2021, almost ten years after we had bought the apartment. It became handy when my son and daughter-in-law left their two children with us for six months in December 2021. For the first time, we used the Puri apartment by going there every month.

Ashiana Lagoon has become a very desirable location now since the new bypass road around Puri connects Bhubaneswar to the beach, just a block away, and it takes only forty-five minutes or less to reach there from the western part of Bhubaneswar. With the new thirteen-storied Swosti hotel next door and the planned new Puri International Airport a few km down the road on the beach, all the regular tourist facilities are now available at the site. We are happy that we spent a couple of years of our valuable time to uplift this common property to the benefit of all owners.

Amruut Foods

A young man with hidden talents and sincerity appeared to sell gardening services for our two buildings in Bhubaneswar. He provided these services to some of the neighbors in our area and also to others in some other neighborhoods in Bhubaneswar. It appeared to us that the service crew that he was bringing from the Balasore area were mostly greenhorns, except for one or two experienced individuals, and that he was not making much of a profit from the services that he was providing at a cheap rate. Finally, he got us a gardener that he had worked with in the Kolkata area, and we provided the gardener to stay in the two rooms where the sangha was being operated. Madhusudan, the gardening contractor, scaled down his gardening contract activities in our area but was row active in the sangha activities. He could sing well, and hence I worked with him to develop the appropriate lyrics for the Prajna Paramita and other sutras used in the Sangha.

Madhusudan later on got interested in small

construction projects that we were undertaking at our two buildings in Bhubaneswar and helped Anuradha, especially when I was not in India. He also gave the lowest bid for the boundary wall construction at Ashiana Lagoon. He got the contract, and then completed the project, and constructed a strong and sound boundary wall. Unfortunately, he lost money because of the contract due to his low bid. It was clear to him now that he could not be successful in that line due to his lack of financial discipline and management. He went back to his home in the Balasore district to establish a sangha and possibly build a Buddhist Zen temple. We helped him on behalf of the sangha by giving away the audio equipment that was procured for the sangha at Bhubaneswar for use at the new sangha. A place was also rented for a while for a sangha. In the meantime, the COVID-19 pandemic surfaced in the year 2020, and all planned meetings stopped. Madhusudan could not engage in sangha activities and make a living.

Anuradha defined for him a pickle product that he could manufacture and sell starting in that area. That is how Amruut Foods started. A pickle of 'Khajoor' or date was defined as a unique product, not generally available anywhere. The brand 'Amruut' was coined for the product, and the operation started. Product labels were prepared, and container bottles were chosen. They were manufactured in an extension room put together next to the home of Madhusudan's parents. The products were sold in the Bhubaneswar and Balasore areas and were very much liked. Other products were added to the list of pickles. I have been an advisor mainly, giving them advice on their strategy, and Anuradha deserves all the credit for the success of this operation.

Amruut Foods has built a building of its own in

the Basta area of Balasore district so that manufacturing and administrative operations will be moved to this new building. Once the interior and exterior finishings are done and the operations move to the new building this year, it would allow Amruut to expand its activities.

The repetitive flood situation in Basta and nearby areas in 2024 and 2025 has made things harder for the construction of the building in Basta and the operation of Amruut Foods. Hopefully, the flood situation will stabilize after the rains, and they can execute their intended plans for relocation and expansion.

19. Revisiting My World

I have now lived through eighty years of my life in India and America. Although I left my village when I was eight years old, I maintained my roots there and often visited my third brother, who lived there with his two sons and their families. Similarly, I maintained my relations at Balangir, the erstwhile capital of the princely state of Balangir Patna. The families of the three sons of my late eldest brother live there, and my classmates from the primary school, high school, and college days are still active there. I have tried to maintain my contacts with friends from NIT and IIT. Though I moved my family in 1997 from America, I kept on visiting the United States a couple of times every year. In this chapter, I wanted to briefly summarize my visits and perspectives regarding these worlds that I am still dreaming along! I divide these into three categories: 1. My Other Places Revisited, 2. Last Trip to America and Some Thoughts, and 3. My Technical World Revisited. I describe in this chapter these revisits to my world.

My Other Places Revisited
Revisiting Bodoboranga

The village of my childhood has changed quite a lot now, and yet many things are still the same as before. Except for a few milking cows in some families needing a constant source of milk, there is no more the morning ritual of cows and the calves gathering in the middle of the village and being led by the cowherd to the pastures surrounding the village. One also misses their coming back in the evening after sunset. The bullocks, which were mostly used for ploughing the land and all other farming activities, have also completely vanished. So, too, we miss the male buffalo, prized for heavy transportation work, especially pulling the carts of people and things to places, near and far. There is not a single bullock cart waiting there now in the middle of the village road.

The river Bahuda, which flows around the village, is now sunken deeper because most of the sand is being taken away for construction purposes. The river banks were used earlier as the approach road to the village. Instead, there is a concrete road now connecting the village to Surangi and Chikiti on one side and to Ichchapuram in Andhra Pradesh on the other side.

Now that all of the villagers have been provided with their latrines, open defecation on the banks of the river is largely eliminated. But the river banks are not clean, and one would find plastics and other garbage around these areas. The Shiva temple and the Radhakrishna mutt are as they were seventy years back. The Thakurani temple has risen to great heights recently with generous funds from the villagers. A Hanuman temple has recently come up at the other end of the village on the bank of the river. The Barahi temple, situated about a kilometer from the village, has a 'Yagnya Mandap' and extension where 'kirtan' and bhajan are performed twenty-four hours since the 1970s. With the support of donations from people belonging to all the surrounding villages, half a dozen people are regularly supported to perform these incessant prayers. Once a year, during the springtime, a mega fair is held at the Barahi site for three days, and people from all around make merry and have entertainment during the evenings. Theatres, plays, songs, and prayers are held throughout this period. Thus, there is no dearth of religious participation by the people around.

Around the year 2004, when a road was constructed connecting the village to the existing road from Surangi to Chikiti, many changes started appearing in the village. First, houses were built outside the village on both sides of this new road. My third brother's two sons built new houses in very wide plots, with the latest kitchen and sanitary facilities, and moved out of the old narrow train compartment-like houses in the main lane of the village.

Around the year 2010, I went back to the village to assess what little I could do to the social fabric of the place as a tribute to it for being the foundation of my life and education. The primary school, which was at my time at the center of the village in a temporary building with a thatched roof, was shifted decades ago to a location on the side of the Shiva temple. It had been upgraded to a school up to class eight, and there was even a new wing where classes could be held if the school was upgraded to the tenth grade and to become a full-fledged high school. The boundary walls of the school were being built, and I was not interested in contributing to that because the government was doing it already. I had noticed that the village had changed a lot. The family cowshed built by my father was all empty, and I was given that as part of my inheritance along with our ancestral house and about six acres of land. I got rid of all this property and wanted to do something worthwhile for the village, as described in a previous chapter, and built Naaree Mahal or the Village Center, as the case may be.

Even after more than seventy years of my leaving the village in the early nineteen fifties, the whole village world is entirely dependent on agriculture for a living. The machines are mostly taking care of the tilling, harvesting, and transportation right now. But the percentage of people engaged in agriculture in the rural areas is still about eighty percent or more. Our whole village has only 750 acres of land for cultivation in the village, giving an average of about five acres per family. This figure has to be at least 25 acres per family in a Viksit Bharat, and that means the village could support only about thirty families in agriculture, and the rest of the families have to move out or be engaged in other activities for their livelihood. So, there is a large superfluous population that has to move to the towns and the cities or find employment nearby within fifty kilometers to stay in the village. This is a dire long-term situation that needs to be addressed by the residents and the government. Those who stay as farmers have to further increase the return from the land of twenty-five acres, in most cases, by innovative methods. This can be addressed if some of these steps are taken:

1. Intensive farming of the land to increase yield and raise other foods like fruits, vegetables, and other products.
2. Establish small and medium food processing industries that are fed from the farm output in the rural area. This would increase the level of income of farming communities.
3. Remove artificial barriers to the process of farm consolidation.

The future of Bodoboranga also depends largely on the development of the surrounding areas. The fact that Patrapur, only one km away, has been recently upgraded to a Notified Area Council (NAC) is a positive thing for further development, though the village does not come under the Patrapur block. The Bahuda Muhana Small Port plan envisioned by the Government of Odisha is a long-term positive for the whole area, since the proposed port would be only about fifteen km away.

Surangi Revisited

A Navodaya High School was established decades ago by the central government adjacent to the palace fort. This has increased the importance of Surangi in the Ganjam district since students from all over the district came to get a high level of education in this central school. There is also a government high school in addition to the original Surangi Primary school, which was there fifty years back and has been upgraded now to a middle school. There are bank branches and other public amenities like medicine stores, post offices, mobile phone sales, and repair centers. The side roads that are connected to the main arterial road of the village are more problematic now compared to earlier times because there is open drainage in the middle of many roads, and one cannot conveniently drive cars through these roads, where most of the villagers live.

The ancestral house belonging to my maternal grandfather is now divided between the five sons of my younger uncle. However, none of them stay in the village since many of their children now work all over the world, in Bengaluru, Kolkata, Bhubaneswar, Atlanta, Detroit, etc. They all have houses built in Berhampur and Bhubaneswar to live there. The land is given to the sharecroppers, and they get some annual income from that. The houses in the village are empty or rented out. This is partly the story of rural India, where the young and the old population of the villages are moving to the adjoining bigger towns for the reason of better communication, employment, health, and education.

Balangir Revisited

Balangir, the erstwhile capital of Balangir Patna state in Odisha, is the headquarters of Balangir district. From 1953 to 1968, it was my hometown. I have visited Balangir every couple of years since then, because many of my relatives and friends were there. My classmates used to hold an annual picnic during the month of December in the town or outside, and I have been able to attend these only occasionally.

A couple of years after I moved from America to Bhubaneswar, I organized a dinner meeting about Balangir at my house in IRC Village, and some of the attendees were:

Vighnaraja Patel, Retired Chief Sec of Odisha, alumnus of PR High School, K.V. Singh Deo, MLA Patnagarh, Maharaja of Balangir Patna, and Bal Gopal Mishra, MLA Loi Singha, alumnus of PR High School.

We did not arrive at any specific action, but agreed to meet later to discuss more on the topic. That was in the year 1999, and we have not met since that day. Nevertheless, Balangir has expanded a great deal during the last sixty years. It was a town of about fifteen thousand, and now it is ten times that at least. The town has expanded in a five-kilometer radius from the center of the town, the district courthouse. Rajendra College, established in 1942 by then King Rajendra N. Singh Deo, is now Rajendra University, offering undergraduate and graduate studies in almost all disciplines, except engineering and medicine. There are some private colleges attached to Sambalpur University. Balangir has become a center of education for the surrounding areas. There are now well-managed private high schools providing secondary education. The government-managed Prithvi Raj High School and Girls' High School have provided education to youths for more than a century now, although they haven't kept up with the earlier high standard of educating the students.

Balangir has become a center of health services for the surrounding areas. Now that a medical college has been established since the year 2021, there will be more developments in this respect. The old district hospital is still providing services to the general public. There are many private health clinics now, and a host of private medical practitioners providing their services, including many of my doctor classmates.

There has been a diploma engineering school since the 1960s. But there is no other engineering educational institute in Balangir or elsewhere in the district. The ordnance factory near Saintala, about 30 km from Balangir on the road to Titlagarh, is the only industrial organization in the district and has been there since the time of Ms. Indira Gandhi.

There is a need for development in many areas at Balangir:
- The original main town and the adjacent areas were planned and executed during the administration of the kingship in the nineteenth and twentieth centuries. But the peripheral areas of the town have organically grown without any proper plans. There are no housing rules and regulations or public drainage systems. The original drainage network connecting the dozen ponds in the town needs to be reclaimed.
- There needs to be small and medium-scale units engaged in the processing and packaging

of agricultural and forest-based products. The educational institutes can also act as entrepreneurial hubs to assist artisans and craftspeople under the PM Viswakarma and other schemes of the Government of India.
- As the Information Technology services industry in India is expanding its operations to second and third-tier cities, Balangir presents a perfect opportunity to attract some of these operations. In that context, the government can establish an STPI (Software Technology Park of India) center in Balangir to train and develop the personnel.
- Balangir district includes many hilly areas where the land is not suitable for cultivation but can be used for solar and wind-based energy production. The government can develop one such center around Balangir to provide further impetus to these kinds of efforts.
- There is a sure need for a sports stadium in the periphery of the city.
- When the Khurdah to Balangir railway line is completed by the year 2026, Balangir could be an important transportation hub connecting the western districts of Odisha. To support tourism around Balangir, there is a need for a multi-purpose entertainment, retail, and conference center in the city, in addition to the hotels that have sprung up in the private sector.
- Balangir is also known for manganese, graphite, and other mines. It is only natural to expect a metal processing industry in the government or private sector.
- Balangir can become an important center in the

country for the design and production of Sambalpuri dresses and sarees.

- It is not far-fetched to wish that the Tusra airport, close to Balangir and completed recently, would have air service soon to Bhubaneswar and other places in India. That would give a big boost to the economy of Balangir.

It is one of my regrets that I have not been able to carry out any concrete personal project for the benefit of the localities in Balangir town, where I lived for a decade. Of course, I was able to provide technical training, employment, and guidance to some of the children of my friends in Balangir through my company in Bhubaneswar.

NIT Revisited

Since relocating back to India from the USA, I have visited NIT Rourkela three to four times, the last time in February 2023, along with a dozen 1968 NIT graduates and their spouses. Though I spent only the first year of engineering at NIT-Rourkela, there was always a strong bond with classmates joining in 1963, because we all stayed in the same hostel and on the three floors of the same south-facing wings and ate at the same cafeteria. I did not know the students who joined the batch in 1964. But I have come to know many of them now living in the Bhubaneswar area since I joined all the activities organized by the 1968 NIT-R association. The group has been regularly holding a general meeting in January of every year in Bhubaneswar, and I have been able to attend all of them.

We had a thorough visit to the whole NIT-R campus during the February 2023 visit. I especially visited the rooms in Hostel 1, where I stayed with three other roommates, each person in one corner of a large room. These rooms were now converted into married student apartments. Further, a completely new wing has been constructed, obstructing the view of the hills. It was nice to be welcomed by the Director of NIT-R himself, and each of us got a memento as part of being the 1968 batch of students. We had a gala evening of entertainment in one of the auditoriums. The hired musical group performed Hindi, Odia, and Sambalpuri songs and dances. Thereafter, some of the talented batchmates had the opportunity to show their musical talents. By the time this was over, all of the batchmates and their spouses tried dancing and twisting their bodies to the tunes rendered. It was an enjoyable evening, and even my wife Anuradha could not help twisting her body for a change!

We also had a trip to Daringbadi later that year with six couples from the NIT-R group. Daringbadi is supposed to be the Kashmir Valley of Odisha! We went to Daringbadi in three Toyota vans and resided there for two nights in a new hotel that had good arrangements for food and rooms. It was a nice drive both ways, going via Berhampur and coming back via the temple darshan at Ladubaba at Odagaon through the route of Kalinga ghats. On the first evening, we visited the highest point of Daringbadi and could see the vast expanse of the valley. We visited the river valleys near the town and enjoyed the sights of the flowing river through the rocky beds. But there is plenty of opportunity to further develop its water parks on the river. The birds and animal amusement park similarly needs more development. Overall, it was a pleasant trip with good food and company.

NIT-R has kept up its reputation as one of the best NITs in India, and is rated as the best technical Institute in Odisha, ahead of IIT Bhubaneswar and many of the private engineering institutes in the state.

IIT Kharagpur Revisited

I had the opportunity to visit IIT Kharagpur in January 2018 to attend the fiftieth anniversary of our graduation. We had an interesting day-long cruise on the river Hooghly in Kolkata with the batchmates and their spouses. There were about a hundred people who had come to attend this event from around the world. Four of my classmates in Electronics were there along with their wives, one from Australia and three from the United States. I was the only one from the electronics batch residing in India. There were many of our batchmates from other branches, especially many of my hostel mates who were from Kolkata. We had two days of various celebrations on campus and had a chance to go around the campus and visit my old hostel, Azad Hall of Residence.

I was pleased to discover that the park area, by the side of which we used to cycle to the Institute from Azad Hall, was extensively developed with a pond and other natural structures to make a beautiful environment. However, I was disappointed looking at the status of the rooms and bathrooms in Azad Hall of Residence.

New buildings have now come up on the main campus to house new departments. I was delighted to know that IIT-Kharagpur had an enrollment of about ten thousand students and expanded into many humanities, sciences, and management departments.

IIT Kharagpur is also participating with private industrial and government-owned organizations to carry out advanced developmental and research activities. This is a very welcome direction compared to earlier times when there was minimal interaction with the industry. The IIT Hospitality Center, where we were housed during the two days of celebrations, was certainly maintained nicely and offered a good impression.

University of Illinois Revisited

I have revisited the University of Illinois at Champaign-Urbana at least half a dozen times since leaving the campus in 1973, after completing my doctoral degree. All of these visits were because I got my son, Arun, admitted there in 1999, to study B.S. in psychology. I used to go and stay in the hotel or with him for at least a week to compensate for being away in India. The campus was almost in the same state as I had left at the time of the 1970s. The Department of Computer Science had rebuilt an impressive new building, replacing the earlier two-story structure. There were a few other new buildings in that part of the campus to house the supercomputer facilities and other new research ventures.

I had met Prof. Bill Kubitz at the Department of Computer Science. I also had tea at the residence of Prof. Braj Kachru and his wife, Prof. Yamuna Kachru of the Department of Linguistics, both of whom I knew during my student days there. My friend and classmate at NIT-Rourkela, Upendra Kachru, was their nephew and completed the MBA at the University of Illinois during my stay there. So, we had many occasions to meet them. I am saddened to learn from Upendra that both of them have departed from the world now.

I was happy that Arun got an overall excellent education at the University of Illinois. He did well in Psychology subjects and was given part-time work at one of the laboratories operated by the department. The laboratory experience showed him that psychology was not something he should pursue as his career, and he decided to prepare to become a medical doctor. It was also beneficial for him to have completed a full set of courses on Hindi offered by the Department of Linguistics so that he was able to read, write, and speak in Hindi. The campus town, Urbana-Champaign, presented a relatively calm atmosphere, far away from the turbulence in Chicago.

New Jersey Revisited

Since I had my house in Branchburg put on a rental lease until the spring of 2018, I used to visit New Jersey every year till then. I used to stay at a central place in a hotel in Piscataway near Route 287, and then visit Branchburg to inspect the condition of the house and arrange for any remedial action. I would also visit close friends living nearby. Here, I attended for the first time the Zen meeting arranged at the Rutgers campus by Professor Spellmeyer in 2013. Subsequently, I had attended the weeklong Zen retreats administered by him in South Jersey in the years 2014 and 2016.

In the spring of 2018, my tenant at the Branchburg house wanted to move out after more than a decade being there. So, I decided to take the opportunity to prepare the house for selling it. I moved there in March and planned extensive remodeling inside and outside so that it would sell fast. The outside cedar shake sidings were ordered to be replaced by Home Depot with vinyl siding. It was executed very late by a Mexican crew, but I was disappointed with Home Depot's handling of the fine points around some unfinished work regarding that. Business ethics had deteriorated in the USA over three decades. I got some of the floorings also changed and got a few of the rooms repainted. It was a quiet time for me living in the empty house for six months, making all the changes. The side trees planted were huge now, after almost four decades. A herd of deer used to come in the afternoon to graze on the big grass lawn. I cut some branches of the trees and fixed my brick patio, done decades ago. My neighbor used to come sometimes to use my dryer. I had plenty of time to do yoga, meditation, and reading.

The plant, where I worked in Somerville, was already razed, and there was a huge food and wine shop with a restaurant and other fancy shops. I visited them at least twice a week to get my groceries. The house was put on the market in July and sold in October. I completed the sale of the house in November and flew to California to visit my son there for a few weeks. That was my last trip to New Jersey.

New Jersey has not changed much during the last three decades of my stay in India, except for the springing up of a few big fancy new malls in Somerville, Bridgewater, and elsewhere. Some of the old malls are partly empty, though.

Massachusetts Revisited

As said earlier, I had sold my last property in Fall River in 2002, and after that, I stayed with my son, Arun, whenever I visited Massachusetts. So, I stayed with him in Worcester, at least a month every year, from 2003 to 2007, when he was in medical school. During the years 2007 to 2010, I stayed with him in Boston during my monthlong visits, where he attended his residency program at Tufts Medical School.

We visited Westborough, Southborough, Marlborough, Shrewsbury, Acton, and other towns to visit friends and attend marriage functions. The last trip was when all of us flew from California to Boston to attend the marriage of Sohini, the younger daughter of Amaresh and Sadhana

Mahapatra. Westborough, our old town where we lived for fifteen years, is almost as it was before. I was surprised to find that Arun had only one of his classmates still living in the town!

Chicago, Louisville, and Davis, Visited

After completing his residency at Tufts, Arun joined the University of Chicago Medical School in Chicago to attend the super specialty program in Pediatric Hematology and Oncology from the years, 2010 to 2013. So, I stayed with him and Swapna in Chicago downtown during my month-long visits every year. I remember visiting the University of Chicago library for their books on Buddhism in the Far East Section. I took their dog Juzi around the blocks where they had rented the two-bedroom apartment. We had the opportunity to dine and wine at a few of the good restaurants in Chicago with their friends.

Arun joined the University of Louisville in Kentucky in the year 2013 as an Assistant Professor, and bought a house in the suburb of the city of Louisville. Swapna resigned from her job in Chicago, and both of them moved to Louisville. Swapna was expecting her first child. So, in the summer of 2013, I flew to Louisville from India. Swapna's parents also drove down there from Cleveland. Swapna gave birth to a baby boy on August 20th, 2013. He was named Arjun Hemant Panigrahi. 'Hema' was the name of my mother and also of Anuradha's mother. So, they had decided to choose this middle name, Hemant.

I visited Louisville during each of the years from 2014 to 2017. In 2015, Anuradha and her mother visited Louisville around the time on April 18th, 2015, when Swapna gave birth to a baby girl. She was named Amrita Sophia Panigrahi. Anuradha's aunt, Emma Padhi from

Canada, also came to Louisville around the same time. So, they all had a good family reunion. Louisville was a small southern city where the people were friendly. I had attended the weekly meetings of a Zen club in the downtown area a few times. I had also attended the celebrations at the local Tibetan temple, where the abbot was someone who had completed his doctoral equivalent degree from the Tibetan University in Karnataka. They had a Tibetan translator who interpreted his teachings into English. The Tibetan Guru Dalai Lama had visited this temple during one of his tours. I visited the Mathematics Professor Ron Sahu and his wife, Sadhna Gupta, a few times in Louisville at their home. I was never there in Louisville at the time of the Kentucky Derby. But the fields were a few blocks away from Arun's house, and we always went there for the evening walk. In the summer of 2017, Arun decided to move to the University of California, Davis. So, I visited him in Davis in November 2018, just after selling my house in New Jersey.

Arun had purchased a four-bedroom ranch house with a large swimming pool in Davis, California. Arjun was attending the public primary school in Davis when he turned five. Amrita was attending a private kindergarten and would also join the public school later. Swapna was staying home and taking care of the kids. During this trip to California, I traveled to Oakland and met my classmate Kiran Rana from IIT Kharagpur. I also talked to my other classmates in Electronics in the Silicon Valley area: Vasan Raman, Parvati Dev, and Kalyan Dutta. Unfortunately, we could not meet due to the impending Thanksgiving vacation in the USA. I went to Shasta Mountain monastery for a weekend Zen retreat. It had very good lodging and meditation facilities on the top of Shasta Mountain, and was led by a dozen resident Bhikshunis and Bhikshus, and followed the Soto Zen tradition adapted for the American environment.

I had a Thanksgiving dinner in the United States after a very long time at Arun's house. His in-laws, who had just moved from Cleveland to the town next to Davis, also joined. I had a chance to look around the wine country and to have dinners at the nice Japanese and other restaurants on the campus in Davis. I visited Sacramento and saw the medical center, where Arun worked. A few days after Thanksgiving, I flew back to Bhubaneswar.

The following year, during the spring of 2019, both Anuradha and I visited Davis and had the chance to spend more time with Arjun and Amrita. We also had plenty of occasions to meet Shastriji and Jyothikaji, Swapna's parents, and visit their new house nearby. Arun took us all in his car to the Los Altos Hills house of Omprakash Agrawal on a Sunday, where we had a great lunch. Arun and Swapna had a chance to meet Omprakash's daughter Anjli, her husband, and her daughter. We met Omprakash and Hema many times in India, whenever they visited Bhubaneswar. But we were visiting them at their house in California after two decades. Driving back from there, we also visited Vinod Rai, his wife, and daughter at their San Jose house. Decades earlier, Vinod lived in Northborough, Massachusetts, and had maintained contact with us.

Last Trip to America and Some Thoughts

Our last trip to the United States was in January 2020 to Hawaii, just before the outbreak of COVID-19. Anuradha and I visited Honolulu after three decades. We stayed a week in a hotel room with a kitchen, just close to the beach. The only difference we noticed was that there were a few green areas on the seashore and a few big new malls on the beach road, where different exotic ethnic foods were available. We saw the big Tesla showroom, where we could see the insides of the Tesla EV.

I have lived in the United States of America for three decades, from 1968 to 1997. During the last three decades, I have been in and out of the USA every year, one or more times. As I look back at the USA from my six decades of experience there, I have the following thoughts.

The United States of America is great not because of the Federal Government in Washington, D.C., but due to the good governance at almost all of the small towns, cities, and states. There is hardly any corruption at the lower levels in the towns, cities, and states. But, as one travels up the ladder, big corruptions happen at the federal level in such a way that they are sanctioned as legally structured by the political lobbying efforts. Some of the glaring examples of gaming and exploiting the system, and other problems in the present American society are:

- The Savings and Loan crisis of the eighties and the nineties, where commercial properties were assigned very high valuations and loans were disbursed widely. Once the property values collapsed, the federal government was persuaded to save the industry by paying about a hundred billion dollars of public money.

- The great financial crisis of 2008 is an example of how the public money was again used to fully bail out Wall Street companies of trillions of dollars.

- Keeping the interest rate almost zero for almost a decade was another situation where Wall Street and the real estate lobby were pandered to at the cost of depositors.

- There is too much control of the government by the financial lobby, and hence, wealth in the society is becoming too concentrated. The tens of billions of dollars in compensation for some of the company executives show the mockery of the system.

- Decades back, when there was a trade deficit of about ten billion dollars with Japan, there was a big push back from the US Congress to set it right. Now there are hundreds of billions of dollars of trade deficits with countries such as China, and nothing happens. No doubt, the deindustrialization of America is happening rapidly.

- The Military Industrial Complex in the USA has too strong a lobby in Washington to keep a war going somewhere so that public money would be spent on that. The wars in Iraq, Afghanistan, and Ukraine are examples of unending wars that continue for years to support this complex.

- Although the USA professes the propagation and support of democratic governments, control and access by the United States government becomes much more important. The use of international aid organizations and NGOs to penetrate inside the political and administrative organs of countries has become a favorite process of the deep state in the United States. The recent events in Bangladesh are an example.

- The health industry in the United States has become too expensive and unreachable for older patients. Anuradha wanted to perform a small surgical operation to remove a benign cyst, but was told to wait six months in the queue. Instead, we got it done at Apollo Hospital in Bhubaneswar under the excellent surgical operation performed by my second brother's grandson. It only cost us a few hundred dollars, whereas it would have cost the same operation almost fifty times more in the US, resulting in at least ten times more from the pocket, even if Medicare pays 80% of the total bill.

- The primary and secondary education provided by the private schools in India now is much better, safer, and far cheaper than what is available in public and private schools in the US. We realized this when my two grandkids got enrolled in the Sai International School in Bhubaneswar during the year 2021. What they learned was much higher than the level provided in the public schools in the city of Davis, California, supposed to be one of the top educated localities in the United States. University education, however, is still better in the United States, compared to what is available in India. But the situation may get better in India as the top institutes in India focus more on research and innovation.

- The regular home services needed for plumbing, electricity, gardening, cleaning, etc., are available in the US at rates fifty times more expensive than in India. Some services, such as cooking, driving, home care, etc., are unavailable and out of reach for the average citizen in the US. That is not the case in India. Elderly patients can stay at home in India and be taken care of when it is not necessary for them to stay in the hospital.

- Undoubtedly, living in India for those aged fifty or higher is much more varied and interesting compared to the living situation in the US. For the younger middle-aged persons who have school-going children, it is also very advantageous to raise the children in the Indian society in an urban setting, provided they have suitable and stable occupational engagements.

- The American society has been on a rapid growth path for the last two hundred years, and only recently started a long-term subminimal growth journey of one to three percent. This is going to bring to the surface many of the buried private racial and cultural feelings against the new successful immigrants who are taking the good jobs!

- Gun violence has accelerated over the years in America, especially due to the easy availability of guns of all kinds. The politicians have not been able to enact laws to control the selling and carrying of guns because of the strong financial muscle of the gun lobby. School children are being the innocent victims. This is a stark failure of American democracy!

- Lastly, the world is going through a rapid realignment process, whereby China and India, with their base of about three billion people, are going to be the top two countries in the world in another quarter century in terms of GDP, military strength, and overall societal wealth. The American empire has already seen its nadir and is only going to go down from here. If there is a future move from the dollar as the premier international currency, that could also lead to a big jolt to American society, considering its extent of the national debt and the loss of freedom to print new money to spend on the military and tide over systemic corruption.

My Technical World Revisited

I often revisit my technical worlds of semiconductors, computers, data networks, AI, and ERP, as the occasions arise. I present here an update of my latest perceptions and views, as I revisit them.

Semiconductor World Revisited

The world of semiconductors has gone through tremendous changes during the last few decades. The semiconductor companies germinated in the nineteen sixties and the seventies and blossomed in the eighties and the nineties as the personal computer revolution spread.

There was further impetus to their expansion with the wide adoption of mobile telephone technology all over the world.

Going forward more than three decades to the present time, the semiconductor and computer industries have gone through profound changes during this time:
1. Intel 32-bit and 64-bit CPU architecture is the predominant version in all personal computers using Microsoft operating system software.
2. Apple Computer has carved out a market share of about 15% using the Apple CPU architecture and Apple operating system software.
3. Special-purpose integrated circuits, such as Graphics Processing Units, have been developed to speed up operations in gaming and other video applications. Companies, such as Nvidia, AMD, Marvel, etc., are the leading vendors.
4. Programmable Logic Devices (PLD) provided a quick way to get a custom LSI device. But a more optimized option was to go the semi-custom way to get an LSI device, whereby customers use the general LSI array offered by a semiconductor fabrication company to customize the upper interconnection layers. Thus, a semi-custom device is relatively quickly obtained at a cheaper rate when compared to a full custom design. As the cost of fabrication of custom devices exploded, most semiconductor companies chose to close their fabs and went the semi-custom route using standard design arrays provided by third-party vendors, such as Taiwan Semiconductor Manufacturing Co (TSMC).

The semiconductor fabrication process has undergone major overhauling during the last many decades. Semiconductor device manufacturing was characterized in the 1980s by process dimensions expressed in 1 micron to 5 microns. Presently, the latest semiconductors are being processed in 1 to 5 nanometers. So, the density of devices has increased by almost six orders of magnitude, or a million times.

The increase in the density and the complexity of the devices had called for a sharp increase in the process complexity and hence the required capital investment. Unless the capital expenses are amortized over the production of a large number of devices, such as microprocessors, graphic processors, etc., companies cannot justify semiconductor plants for the manufacturing of a small number of LSI devices.

In the eighties and the nineties, all the semiconductor companies had their semiconductor fabrication facilities, and they were all integrated device manufacturers. Even many computer companies, such as IBM and Digital Equipment, etc. had their semiconductor divisions for designing and producing the semiconductor devices that were based upon their computer system architecture. As the complexity of semiconductor chip manufacturing increased, each new fabrication plant required investments in the range of five to twenty billion dollars.

This scale of investment was untenable for the computer systems companies, which did not have the high component volume to amortize their investment. Consequently, all system manufacturers, one by one, closed their semiconductor divisions and went for manufacturing the special devices from outside. Sperry, Univac, NCR, Burroughs, and Digital Equipment Corporation closed their semiconductor operations. Finally, IBM also downsized the semiconductor fabrication facilities.

Economics of large scale became also applicable

to the semiconductor companies as the complexity of semiconductor fabrication techniques increased. Most of them became fabless semiconductor design and support companies, except for a few large and specialized companies, such as Intel, Microchip, Analog Devices, Texas Instruments, and ON. These can be called Integrated Device Manufacturers, or IDM. Of course, there are a bunch of such semiconductor companies in Europe (STM, Bosch, Infineon, NXP) and Asia (Samsung, Mitsubishi, Sony, etc.) because of different economies of scale, size, diversity, and government support.

The semiconductor and component divisions of the computer system companies where I worked were all gone decades ago. The pure semiconductor division of RCA Solid State, where I worked, was sold to Harris Semiconductors, and they closed the whole manufacturing plant after extracting the technology and the markets. In that very place, a huge marketing complex of stores, restaurants, and sales offices points to 'de-manufacturing' of the United States of America. Of course, the process started in the 1980s when the dollar became so expensive that most electronics industries migrated to Asia, and thereby the economy of diversification vanished. The pendulum swung now to the other extreme, such that there was the danger of having no IDMs anymore in the United States of America. Hence, the CHIPs Act of the USA aims to assist Intel and other semiconductor companies to invest in their fab centers in the USA.

Coming back to India, it is a dream come true that under the India Semiconductor Mission (ISM), the Government of India has now allotted an amount of ten billion dollars towards supporting semiconductor manufacturing Industries in India as a first step. Consequently, Micron, the semiconductor memory manufacturing company from the USA, is in the process of setting up an Assembly, Test, Marking, and Packaging (ATMP) plant in Sanand. Tata Group has announced the plan to set up an ATMP plant in Assam. Undoubtedly, others will follow in this path of in-house and outsourced test and packaging business.

Even more important is the fact that Tata Electronics, collaborating with Power Chip of Taiwan, has announced the plan to establish a modern semiconductor fabrication plant in Dholera, Gujarat, at a cost estimate of twenty-one billion dollars, with the Government of India contributing half of that as part of production-linked Incentives (PLI). Other Indian companies, such as CG Power, Keyner Technology, L& T Semiconductor, etc. also exploring the possibility of investing in the semiconductor Industry. Once India manufactures the integrated circuits in volume in India, the pace of development in electronics will explode!

It is especially delightful for me to learn that Bhubaneswar is going to have a silicon-carbide wafer processing company and another company focusing on the assembly and packaging of chips. The government of Odisha is projecting Bhubaneswar and Odisha as a center for semiconductors and is attracting more public and private investment in this key area. The local universities and institutes, such as IIT Bhubaneswar, NIT Rourkela. And others are getting roped into the research and development projects relating to semiconductors.

World of Computers Revisited

The world of the computer has gone through tremendous changes in the last few decades. When I started working at Burroughs Corporation, there were IBM and the five bunch (Burroughs, Sperry, Univac, NCR, and CDC), which ruled the mainframe computer market. Of these, only IBM is competing in the same market now. NCR is no longer in mainframe computers but sells specialized financial transaction-based systems. All other companies have been directly or indirectly absorbed into Unisys. All of the minicomputer companies (Digital Equipment Corporation, Data General, Wang, Hewlett-Packard, etc.) have been absorbed into HP Enterprises or vanished. The personal computer companies proliferating in the 1980s are now largely limited to HPQ, Dell, and Lenovo (IBM PC Division). Apple also sells its line of personal computers.

Burroughs Corporation is absorbed into Unisys, and there is hardly any trace of Unisys now in the New Jersey area of the United States of America. Digital Equipment Corporation is largely integrated now into HP Enterprise. The myriads of engineering and manufacturing organizations used by Digital Equipment in the Massachusetts area have vanished. Having worked at Digital Equipment for about eleven years, I get a retirement income from HPE, the remaining entity.

Coming back to the Indian scene, there is no Indian mission to develop mainframe computers or servers, and the commercially available IBM, Unisys, HPE, or other PC-based server systems are used. In the personal computer area, HP, Dell, Lenovo, and other systems (Acer, Toshiba, etc.) are readily available. So are the Apple personal computers. To encourage local manufacturing of personal computer systems and laptops, the Government of India is rightly pushing all the players to do so by a mix of import duties and subsidies.

The Government of India should keep funding the development of Supercomputers, which could be developed largely with the help of commercially available CPU and GPU chips.

The 'Quantum Machines' initiative by the Government of India is a laudable one to leapfrog technology and establish leadership in this new field. The central government must increase research and development in these and other promising areas to sustain global leadership.

Networking World Revisited

I started my journey in the networking world with my graduation project in pulse code modulation (PCM) systems in the Communications Laboratory of IIT Kharagpur. The next stop was the giant nationwide data network project envisioned in the 1970s by MaBell as part of a systems group in Bell Telephone Laboratories for three years. After an interval of about a dozen years, I worked as a marketing product manager in the personal computer networking area at Digital Equipment Corporation, and then the three years at Process Software Corporation as the head of engineering in the development of TCP/IP network for VAX/VMS systems and the development of the web server system for Windows NT systems. Thus, I had a wide-ranging experience spanning many decades in various roles in large and small companies, and consider this area also as the backbone of my technical world.

Things have moved very fast in the last decades here. Surprisingly enough, there is not a single North American company anymore designing, manufacturing, and marketing telecommunication data networking gear. Western Electronics and Aliant Networks of the Bell Systems are gone. So is Northern Telecom of Canada. Nokia of Finland and Ericson of Sweden are the only two companies providing telecom data gear in America,

Europe, and elsewhere. Huwae of China and Samsung of South Korea provide these gears all over the world, but Huwae is banned by most of the Western countries and India for security.

4G and 5G networks have been widely employed in the Western world and India. It is heartening to note that India is taking leadership in the installation of 6G networks, and Indian companies have developed the hardware and software gear associated with these deployments.

There is only a single large networking company left among the American companies, namely Cisco Systems. This is the only networking gear and service company that has survived in the competitive landscape, and Cisco only makes the switching and routing components required at the periphery and not the backbone transmission networks.

It is heartening to know that India has widely employed 5G networks now and, leading in the development and research relating to 6G networks. At my Bhubaneswar house, I have had a 5G connection for a while, and that provides me the internet services, including streaming for the television services offered from around the world.

AI World Revisited

The world of artificial intelligence has been a rage in the years 2023 and 2024, especially after the release of ChatGPT. The eighties and the nineties saw the adaptation of the 'expert systems' AI technology for the automation and/or the augmentation of agents for financial services: Insurance agents for policy analysis, stock brokers for stock selection, and analysts for market analysis, etc. Expert systems were also employed selectively in the automation of certain manufacturing steps, for example, system configurations as per customer requirements were done automatically at DEC.

The present rage in AI relates to 'artificial general intelligence'. Corporations believe that such intelligence would be used by everyone to augment their daily activities. It is believed that there is a great demand for using such intelligence not only in search operations but also in all the processes where decisions are made. Just as in earlier stages of AI adoption, this time too, the biggest impacts would be in agentic applications in the areas of finance, marketing, and health. However, it will be on a much wider scale.

The central and state governments in India need to assist in the development of Large Language Models (LLM) and Small Language Models (SLM) for large-scale applications. India must have AI and internet tools in vernacular languages for safeguarding the sovereignty of the nation. It is the reality that the private software companies in India have not made much headway in software product development and marketing. Hence, the central government must bring in special incentives to help develop a toolset of software applications, including AI applications.

ERP World Revisited

The Enterprise Resource Planning (ERP) world had a tectonic shift with the introduction of the Software as a Service (SaaS) model, where vendors provide cloud-based ERP services, which are subscription-based. This has allowed for central management of the data and infrastructure, and most importantly, allows for scaling of the services as the organization expands and the needs change. A few new players, such as Salesforce and Zoho, etc. are providing these services in addition to the traditional ERP software companies, such as SAP, Oracle, Etc.

The implementation of ERP in Indian organizations has become more widespread as the businesses have become more performance and efficiency- centric in a competitive environment.

The most urgent need today to guarantee our digital independence is the development of an internet tool set in Indian languages. The Government of India must support the development of browsers and search engines in Indian languages.

There is an urgent area relating to enterprise tools, such as mail, composition, presentation, teamwork, project management, etc., where the central and state governments can establish a supporting environment to develop these tools in Indian languages. ERP and other tools should be developed in Indian languages. This cannot happen unless the government provides financial and other forms of subsidy, and uses these in all government operations.

Entrepreneurship Revisited

As I look back on my years of technical entrepreneurship in India, it is clear to me that I tried many possible marketing areas that were within my capabilities and experiences. Of course, I anchored my activities to Bhubaneswar and the surrounding market within about 500km. The IT service and/or software development service market that I had hoped for in the United States never materialized due to the lack of marketing muscle, experience, and interest in that specific area.

An office in Kolkata was managed for a couple of years and was supported by personnel from Bhubaneswar, but, was not fruitful. The software training market provided critical skills to graduating engineers, but, was not sustainable to provide high-quality training at minimal charges. The computer system and networking hardware services business could have been profitable only if there were some orders from the government organizations. This was not attained because of our transparent business practices. The ERP software business did not take off since most customers at the time did not have urgent performance needs or had the approved budgets to implement the solutions, and hence, we wasted valuable time showing them small custom solutions.

Custom software development was only profitable if the company could learn from the experience to develop generic software products for the larger overall market. Our development of Exam Pro test software was one such product, and we could not scale it up to generate volume.

Similarly, the Materials Management Software applications developed for Paradeep Phosphates Ltd. In Odisha was a very useful tool for the customers, but we could not generalize it to market to the larger market.

This was the time before the start of the trend to sell software as a service (SaaS). We could have repositioned our examination applications and specialized ERP applications as online software services for customers! In summary, we could not adapt to the changing market needs.

Our focus on the development of products was due to my own experience entirely in the areas of advanced product development and marketing. But it was somewhat premature in the Indian market three decades back, and especially from a city like Bhubaneswar at the time. Product development requires focus and big investments in a sustained manner. We lacked both.

So, one of the big impediments to the success of the enterprise was the lack of outside investment apart from the two entrepreneurs in a conjugal relationship. Both of them gave up more than a dozen years of their life without taking any remuneration and even provided free quarters and electricity for the company during the entire duration. This was ultimately not a healthy corporate arrangement! But the entrepreneurs could say that they gave everything and tried their best to succeed in this path! We helped hundreds of students in their training and provided opportunities in Bhubaneswar for tens of software engineers to be engaged in software development. We pioneered the automation of the examination process in Odisha and helped perform the ERP implementations. So, we helped Odisha and India in our small ways! Fortunately, the investments that we had made in the construction of the two buildings in India have appreciated a great deal and continue to provide us comfort in retirement life, and also generate some continuing rental income.

World of Engineering Education Revisited

BIET, the Engineering College where I worked briefly in the year 2000, is still operating as a private institution in the Bhadrak area of Odisha. I had been a member of the governing board for some years, but did not have any more contact during the last decade.

Biju Patnaik National State Institute (BPNSI), where I worked for about a year, was appropriately shifted from Puri to the Kalinga Nagar area, the primary hub of steel technology in Odisha. It is mainly concentrating now on developing skilled manpower in support of the steel industry.

The management of engineering education, especially in private institutions, was never transparent, and for them to grow into top world institutions, there must be better rules, regulations, and audits of these institutions. Governance must be efficient, transparent, and altruistic. They should never be just the private domain of a few individuals, but must be publicly transparent. For them to grow up to be citadels of learning, there must be ideals of service to society rather than private profit and individual prosperity.

20. The Road to Nirvana!

As I sit to write in the eighty-first year of my life, the road ahead looks straight and uncomplicated! An end is coming, but not yet. Until that instant of loss of consciousness, life will be lived and appreciated for what it is, since that is the greatest gift one has, to sense this world and live and let live!

In this last chapter of the book, I describe my transformed city of Bhubaneswar and how I have spent my retirement years while living here. I describe how I spend time every day at this stage of life. Lastly, I talk about my plan to walk on the path for the remaining years.

My Small Beautiful City

To describe my present life, I must describe first my small city of Bhubaneswar, where I have lived for almost three decades after moving back from America. Bhubaneswar has evolved during the last three decades to be a very desirable and beautiful small city in India.

From a small town with a population of only about fifteen thousand in the nineteen fifties, it has grown now to have a population of more than a million residents. The greater capital region, including Cuttack, Khurdah, and Pipili, has a population of about three million. This much population, spread out over non-congested areas, gives enough marketing muscle to draw major events to this arena. Of course, if I add Puri with its beaches and the planned international airport to the above capital cluster, it becomes a bigger city. That would be a reality when the planned Bhubaneswar Metro Network is extended to include all of these major population centers. The recently announced Ring Road project around Bhubaneswar and Cuttack further plans to integrate Dhenkanal, Choudwar, and Banki into the capital region. The plans are on the anvil for a mega metro city of the future!

Bhubaneswar itself is rated in India to be the second most beautiful small city of India, next only to Simla in Himachal Pradesh. A recent United Nations organization rated Bhubaneswar as the most livable city in Asia, considering its wide greenery and uncongested road network. Bhubaneswar does not have any manufacturing industry in or around the city, and hence, there is no question of pollution from them. Pollution due to vehicular traffic is also minimal. The city gets a nice sea breeze coming in most afternoons to make life bearable in summer. The northwestern part, where VIP Colony is located in Bhubaneswar, is at least five degrees cooler due to being next to the park and having the jungles beyond the park.

Bhubaneswar has become a big center for education and health. The following universities and institutes are located in Bhubaneswar or nearby areas:

Utkal University, Bhubaneswar

Utkal University of Culture (UUC), Bhubaneswar

Rama Devi Women's University, Bhubaneswar

Odisha University of Agriculture & Technology (OUAT), Bhubaneswar

Indian Institute of Technology (IIT), Bhubaneswar

The International Institute of Information Technology (IIIT), Bhubaneswar

National Institute of Science Education and Research (NISER), Bhubaneswar

All India Institute of Medical Sciences (AIIMS), Bhubaneswar

Ravenshaw University, Cuttack

Kalinga Institute of Industrial Technology (KIIT) University, Bhubaneswar

Shiksha O Anusandhan (SOA) Deemed University, Bhubaneswar

Sri Sri University (SSU), Cuttack

XIM University, Bhubaneswar

Institute of Mathematics & Applications (IMA), Bhubaneswar

Institute of Physics, Bhubaneswar

Institute of Life Sciences (ILS), Bhubaneswar

Sriram Chandra Bhanja (SCB) Medical College, Cuttack

CV Raman Global University, Bhubaneswar

National Law University Odisha, Cuttack

Bhubaneswar also has more than two dozen engineering colleges that are affiliated with the Biju Patnaik University of Technology (BPUT). A dozen engineering diploma colleges are located in Bhubaneswar. A good number of management schools are also located around Bhubaneswar.

Bhubaneswar has medical colleges, such as SCB College of Cuttack, which are affiliated with Odisha University of Health Sciences. KIIT University has the Kalinga Institute of Medical Sciences (KIMS) and a hospital affiliated with it. SOA Deemed University has the Institute of Medical Sciences (IMS) and a hospital associated with it.

The Integrated Global Financial Technology Capability Hub (I-GFTCH), BharatNetra, was launched recently at Bhubaneswar and has a collaboration with Global Finance and Technology Network (GFTN), National

University of Singapore (NUS), and Asian Institute of Digital Finance (AIDF). This would bring in more financial companies to Bhubaneswar.

In the case of school education, some leading schools of global standard are: Sai International School, KIIT International School, Delhi Public School, Birla International School, and many others.

The following reputed private hospitals are also operating in Bhubaneswar: Apollo Hospital and Cancer Center, CARE Hospital, Kalinga Hospital, Bagchi Cancer Center, L V Prasad Eye Hospital, Tata Cancer Hospital, and many other large and mid-size hospitals.

At least half a dozen very big and small shopping plazas have been operating around Bhubaneswar and offer good opportunities for shopping and entertainment. We use the Esplanade Plaza on the Cuttack Road and the Pal Heights Plaza in Nayapally to do shopping and to watch the latest movies. The Smart Bazaar in Krishna Plaza in Nayapally allows me to do the weekly groceries, while having the car in the underground garage. This is supremely more convenient than the big outside parking lots in the suburban areas in the United States.

A variety of new restaurants have opened around Bhubaneswar in the last decades to cater to the tastes of the young and old residents. There are now all the fast-food chains operating in Bhubaneswar. But restaurants offering Thai, Japanese, Continental, and other specialized cuisines are also operating now in Bhubaneswar. There are more than two dozen large hotels in Bhubaneswar that provide restaurants and the marriage/party mandap facilities.

In terms of sightseeing, recreation, and entertainment, the following stand out around Bhubaneswar:

Nandankanan Zoo and Park

Khandagiri Caves
Lingaraj Temple
Raja Rani Temple and many other temples of Old Bhubaneswar
Ekamrakanan Park, with lakes, a cactus garden, and flower gardens
Buddhist Peace Pagoda at Dhauli
Rabindra Mandap, where plays, dances, and musicals are held
Bhanja Kala Mandap, where plays, dances, and musicals are held
Bhubaneswar Museum
Science Museum, Bhubaneswar
Pathani Samanta Planetarium, Bhubaneswar
Lalitagiri, Ratnagiri, and Udayagiri Buddhist sites near Jajpur
Kalinga Stadium, where the world hockey tournaments are held
Barabati Stadium in Cuttack, where cricket tournaments are held

During the last three decades, Bhubaneswar has expanded almost to Cuttack in the north and Pipili in the south on the road to Puri. The road network around the city has improved greatly. A New Bhubaneswar Railway station has been added, and the Bhubaneswar Railway station is going through a major upgrade. Bhubaneswar Airport has a new terminal and is being further expanded, and the plans are to connect it to the Metro Network. A large convention center is also being developed by the state government. Info Valley, the second IT Park on the outskirts of Bhubaneswar, is drawing more companies to Bhubaneswar. In summary, Bhubaneswar has transformed itself into a nice small city in India. So, living in Bhubaneswar has become a pleasure in terms of educational opportunities, health facilities, entertainment avenues, and overall wellness.

Trips in India and Abroad

I have now lived almost fifteen years in the so-called retirement. But in reality, I am busier than ever. The amount of travel has reduced, especially after the COVID-19 pandemic. Here I will describe some of the trips in India and abroad that we have been busy with, besides all the projects and plans described in the earlier chapters in Part IV. Many of these trips have been educational in guiding my life further, especially as a Zen Buddhist.

Sikkim and Darjeeling Trips

We were certainly occupied with different responsibilities relating to the daily operation of PanNet, and hence, it was always difficult to take vacations within and outside of India. Now that we were not entangled in the company affairs, we took a trip in May 2010 to Sikkim and the surrounding areas in the northeast of India. We went all the way to Nathula Pass at about eighteen thousand feet high on the border of Tibet. It was a scenic drive on a very narrow road cut through the mountains. The services provided by the Nepali serviceman in the hotel were excellent. Gangtok, the capital of Sikkim, was beautifully situated and provided plenty of evening entertainment and dining facilities.

The trip to Darjeeling was also enjoyable. We were surprised that it was so cold even in summer. The early morning view of Kanchenjunga from the hills of Darjeeling was brilliant and unforgettable. We visited a few of the Buddhist temples in Darjeeling. They were all from the Vajrayana sect, catering to the Nepali people. The Darjeeling markets had many artifacts and silver jewelry on display, and Anuradha picked up some.

Bengaluru and Mysuru Trip

Another time in September 2011, on my trip back from the United States, I flew to Bengaluru International Airport. Anuradha joined me from Bhubaneswar. We stayed in Bengaluru for a few days and visited the different landmarks. I had not visited Bengaluru since my summer training days in 1967. Bengaluru had changed immensely compared to those days. I was sorry to see that Caban Park no longer presented the pristine green and serene environment. The Mahatma Gandhi Road area was unrecognizable. We visited the ashram of Sri Ravisankar and were impressed by the scale of the facilities. The ISKN temple on the hill had just started at that time, but had an impressive plan to build the tallest structure in Bengaluru. We traveled to Mysuru by train and spent a few days there. The Mysore Palace was very impressive from the outside and inside. The lighting of the palace was a sight to see and feel in the evening! We visited the Vrindavan Gardens near Mysuru, and had a whole day and evening of pleasure looking at the water parks and the lights.

Rajasthan Trip

In September 2012, while I was coming back from a trip to the United States, Anuradha joined me in New Delhi, flying from Bhubaneswar. We embarked on an elaborate trip to Rajasthan. From New Delhi, we took an overnight train journey to Jaisalmer and saw the historical merchant houses and other regular houses still used by residents inside the fort area. The camel rides in the nearby deserts and the evening entertainment, and dinner under the open sky were memorable events. So were the views of some of the temples, especially the Jain temples around Jaisalmer.

From Jaisalmer, we went to Jodhpur by train, and saw the great Jodhpur fort and then the Jodhpur palace. Our next train stop was Ajmer, where we saw the lakefront garden and forts built by the Mughal emperors. The visit to the Ajmer Dargah was a special treat, but, did not like the almost choking rush inside the central hall. From Ajmer, we took the train to a stop near Mt. Abu and took a taxi to the city. Mt. Abu is a beautiful city tucked around the mountains and lakes. We saw the campus of the Brahmakumaris and took the rides on the lakes. We visited a famous Jain temple near there, which was high on the hills and had the statue of all the Tirthankaras.

From Mt. Abu, we went to Udaipur and stayed overlooking a nearby lake. We saw the Udaipur palace, situated by the side of the lake. We went up to the small palace built on top of the mountain, where water harvesting techniques were used to ensure the availability of water on the mountain top. A beautiful view of this city of lakes was presented from the vantage point at the palace. Udaipur also has a few great temples with elaborate architecture and places for the entertainment of the tourists.

From Udaipur, we flew to Jaipur, and saw the Jaipur Palace, and another old palace on the outskirts of the city on a mountain top. There was plenty of opportunity to buy Rajasthani artifacts and textiles. We brought home a few for us and Arun. We flew back from there to Bhubaneswar through Delhi.

Kerala Trip

Anuradha planned a trip to Kerala in December 2014. We flew to Hyderabad and stayed there overnight, and then flew to Cochin International Airport from there. We stayed in Ernakulam for a couple of days and visited Kochi downtown by crossing the waterways by the steamers. We took a relaxing walk through the Jewish synagogue, the gift shops, the temples, and finally enjoyed the mesmerizing Kathakali and South Indian classical dances and martial arts at Kathakali Center at Fort Kochi. The sea shores in Fort Kochi and Ernakulam presented a cool environment to walk around. The various churches, such as Santa Cruz Cathedral, St. George's Church, etc., presented excellent views.

We took the train from Ernakulam to Thiruvananthapuram and stayed there for a few days. We went to Kovalam beach and relaxed by enjoying the sights and sounds. The visit to the Padmanabhaswamy temple was a memorable one. This is supposed to be the richest temple in the world and has a vast store of gold and diamonds donated by the devotees, including the royalty of Travancore. We also took a day trip to a Kerala green journey arranged by the tourism department. We traveled by car and then had boat rides through the streams in a rural community, and had an authentic Keralite lunch. We had a day-long trip to Kanyakumari by bus. The visit to the Vivekananda Rock Memorial, in the sea at the confluence of the three seas, the Bay of Bengal, the Arabian Sea, and the Indian Ocean, was the culmination of this trip.

We took the train to Alappuzha next for our houseboat trip in the Kerala backwaters. It was a splendid experience at the boathouse, slowly cruising through the lake, while sitting on the upper deck and having a Keralite lunch consisting of grilled fish and other niceties. We roamed around the lake until the evening and then anchored at an island boat stop, where we had the chance to walk out of the boat and enjoy a dinner at the restaurants there. After the dinner, we came back to the boat to rest for the night. The next morning, we travel back the way in the morning sun.

Our next destination was Kollam, where we went to the beach in the evening. The next day, we traveled back to Cochin Airport and then flew to Hyderabad. A day was spent roaming around Charminar and the Golkonda fort areas. Another day was spent at the Ramoji Studio on the outskirts of Hyderabad. There were plenty of different shows and gardens to go through there. After this short two-day visit to Hyderabad, we flew back to Bhubaneswar.

Malaysia and Vietnam Trip

In the year 2015, we flew to Kuala Lumpur from Bhubaneswar and spent a few days there looking around the city and the nearby areas. The Petronas Twin Towers area was an obvious choice to look at on the first day, especially since it was not very far from our hotel. The next morning, we saw Batu Caves, made out of limestone deposits, and where there were some Hindu shrines. After further sightseeing and shopping in Kuala Lumpur, we left for the airport, and on the way, saw the city of Putrajaya, the administrative center of Malaysia. The city has splendid mosques, palaces, and government buildings, neatly situated around lakes and bridges.

We flew to Ho Chi Min City from the airport. We saw the Old Central Post Office, the War Remnants Museum, and the Notre Dame Cathedral. The next day, we visited the Saigon River delta to experience the suburban and rural Vietnamese life, and how they lived and carried on business around the water bodies. We had plenty of opportunities to taste the Vietnamese food in the city markets and restaurants.

We flew to Hanoi from Ho Chi Min. The hotel in Hanoi was overlooking a large lake at the back, and the people there were so friendly and helpful. To avoid getting late for the show in the evening, they took us on their two-wheelers to avoid the rush. There was the Thang Long water puppet show depicting the history of the people. We saw the Ho Chi Min Mausoleum and the B52 Victory Museum, and the Hanoi Flag Tower. The next morning, we travel by road to Ha Long Bay and go on the boat there, exploring the many caves. The scenes on the water are unlike anywhere else in the world, with hundreds of rocks in between the waterways. We travel back to Hanoi at the end of a busy day in Ha Long Bay. We have more Vietnamese food in the evening and the next day in the city, and then fly out east through the Middle East to the United States to visit Arun in Louisville, Kentucky.

Trip to Varanasi, Sarnath, and Bodhgaya

In September 2015, I took a trip alone to Varanasi, Sarnath, and Bodhgaya to see firsthand the places associated with the Buddha, as a step towards knowing his life's journey. I flew to Varanasi from Bhubaneswar via Kolkata. I spent a night at a hotel on the side of the river Ganga. The next morning, I walked from my hotel room to the ghat underneath and walked north all the way to Assi Ghat. The Ghats were quite clean and had no trouble walking from one to the other. Near the Assi Ghat at the upper level, there was a decorated pandal, where there was live music, and a place to sit down and enjoy the serenity of the place. I took a taxi to Sarnath that day and stayed there for two nights.

Sarnath has been restored now to a certain extent,

and I could see the Dhamek Stupa, where the Buddha gave his first sermon to the five disciples. I saw the Mulagandhi Kuti, where Buddha built the shelter for the first rain retreat. I saw the temples and shrines built by some of the Buddhist countries there.

I went by train to Gaya from Varanasi and then by taxi to Bodhgaya, and stayed there for three nights. I saw the Mahabodhi Temple Complex and the Bodhi Tree, under which the Buddha obtained enlightenment. There are plenty of temples, shrines, and meditation centers here, built by every Buddhist country and many Buddhist organizations at this holiest site of Buddhism. I sat in meditation under the Bodhi Tree. I walked over the Sujata Bridge over the river Niranjana to the other side in one evening and could feel the serenity of the river. I took a day trip to Rajgir and Nalanda from Bodhgaya by car. I saw at Rajgir the Venu Vana, which King Bimbisara had donated to the Buddha and where the Buddha stayed. I could also see the Gridhrakuta Mountain cave of the Buddha from there. I visited the relics of Nalanda Vihar after driving to Nalanda. It was an eye-opening understanding of how the teachers discussed and taught the topics of the day. I went to see the new Nalanda International University that was being built at Rajgir with financial support from the world community. The next day, I took the train back to Varanasi and then flew back to Bhubaneswar. It was a very enlightening trip to see and feel the Buddha. I was ready to write my story of the Buddha now.

Zen Trip to Japan

I took a solitary trip to Japan in January 2018, right after the Fifty-Year IIT meet at Kharagpur. Since Anuradha had to take care of her ailing mother, I went alone to discover firsthand the Zen monasteries of Japan, especially the ones from the Rinzai Zen sect. I had to get a Japanese Visa by going to the Kolkata Consulate with return tickets to India. I flew from Bhubaneswar to Kuala Lumpur and from there to Haneda International Airport near Tokyo. I had seen Tokyo in the year 1986, when I had a business trip to all of the Japanese Semiconductor companies, as described earlier. I took the train from Haneda to Kamakura on the coast and stayed there the night, and early morning, I saw the giant Buddha of Kamakura. From there, I walked to the Engaku-ji Monastery, where the famous Zen writer D.T. Suzuki had stayed. It is a huge monastery by the side of a mountain and has many large meditation halls, Zen gardens, and residential quarters for the hermits. Kencho-ji is the other Rinzai monastery in Kamakura, and I spent the rest of the day visiting there. It is at least as big a Zen monastery as Engaku-ji, and has large meditation halls, temples, and gardens.

From Kamakura, I went back to Haneda by train and then flew to Osaka's Kansai International Airport. I stayed in Osaka for a day to see the famous Osaka Castle and move around the city. The next day, I took the train to Kyoto and stayed in the city for three days to see the important Rinzai Zen temples and other important landmarks of Kyoto. I saw the Kyoto Imperial Palace and the gardens. I visited the following monasteries:

Myoshin-ji, established in 1342 by Emperor Hanazono, with fifty sub-temples and the Zen gardens nationally designated place of beauty, Head Temple of the Rinzai sect with four thousand temples affiliated worldwide.

Nanzen-ji, established in 1291 by Emperor Kameyama, Head Temple.

Tofuku-ji has some of the best Zen gardens.

Kenin-ji was founded by Eisai in 1202 and is the oldest Zen temple in Japan.

Tenryu-ji has many Zen gardens of exquisite beauty.

Kyoto has many other famous temples of other Buddhist sects, and I did not have the time to see them. Kyoto is also the center of the Japanese film industry and is one of the most beautiful cities in the world. From Kyoto, I took the Shinkansen to Tokyo and then flew back to Bhubaneswar from Haneda. This was definitely a trip to remember, although the weather was cold and snowy in Kyoto. It would be worthwhile visiting Kyoto again in spring, when the cherries bloom.

Thailand Trip

While traveling back from Honolulu to India in January 2020, we flew from Osaka Kansai Airport to Phuket in Thailand. Anuradha had not been to Thailand and had arranged this trip to Phuket, Pattaya, and Bangkok. Phuket, on the west coast of Thailand, was a beach town, full of sights and shows. There was a busy market on the beach street, where you could buy many things from this part of the world and bathe in the sun or water on the beach. We visited the Big Buddha on Nakkerd Hills and explored other sights in Phuket. One evening was spent attending the Simon Cabaret show with the team of ladyboys dressed elaborately and performing like in Las Vegas.

We flew to Pattaya on the east coast of Thailand and spent two days exploring the boat rides and island hopping. Pattaya offered many restaurants with Indian and Thai cuisines that we enjoyed during our stay there. We took a taxi ride from Pattaya to Bangkok and stayed in a hotel on the side of the Chao Phraya River. We visited the Grand Palace and the temple Wat Phra Kaew in there. We also saw the temple Wat Pho, where there is the reclining Buddha statue, and Wat Arun for the rising sun. All of these places were close to the river, and one could walk there after crossing the river by boat. We also looked at the markets and enjoyed the restaurants overlooking the river.

We flew back to Kolkata from Bangkok in the first week of February, and they were already checking the incoming passengers for COVID-19.

Retirement Life

Retirement life has undoubtedly offered more flexibility in the planning of our domestic responsibilities. Otherwise, we could not have taken all the trips mentioned above. It also offers us the opportunity to participate more in family get-togethers and ceremonies, and other hobbies and interests, as described here as a good part of our retirement life.

Family and Friends

We have attended most of the family ceremonies held in Bhubaneswar, Cuttack, Puri, Berhampur, and Balangir in Odisha. We have also attended a few of the ceremonies held in Kolkata and elsewhere by family friends. I was able to attend the marriage of my IIT classmate Ramamurthy's daughter in Mumbai in 2013. We were also delighted when Ramu visited us in 2015 along with his wife and her sisters. As told earlier, I was also able to attend the marriage of Sohini, daughter of Amaresh and Sadhna Mahapatra, in Massachusetts, along with Arun, Swapna, Arjun, and Amrita.

There are a couple of ceremonies every year for one or more grandchildren of my three elder brothers and my sister, and of my cousin brothers and sisters. Similarly,

Anuradha has her sister and many cousins. So, we always attend the family ceremonies, the marriages, the sacred thread ceremonies, birthdays, the marriage anniversaries, and lately, many Shraddha ceremonies. That is one good thing about living in Bhubaneswar, whereby we could attend most of the family ceremonies around Odisha. For the three decades, when I was in the USA, I did not have this opportunity. I was not able to attend the Shraddha ceremonies when my mother died in 1985 and my eldest brother died in 1987, both in Balangir.

I was there when my second brother, Padmanna, died in Berhampur in 2015, and my sister, Subasa Abba, died in 2010. More recently, when my third brother, Rupanna, died in January 2025, I was able to attend the whole Shraddha ceremony in Bodoboranga. We also attended Shraddha ceremonies when Anuradha's mother's two sisters and their husbands died in Puri during the last decade. There have been Shraddha ceremonies for other departed relatives and friends in Bhubaneswar and Puri, and we were able to attend them.

Internet, Television, and News

There is no doubt that I spend more time now on the internet than before. I try to limit it often by checking the mail as one of the last activities after other work. There is, of course, more reading of the news on the internet rather than the television, since most of the shows are combative rather than being informative. The morning newspapers, Times of India and Dharitri (Odia Daily), give me a quick view of the world around during breakfast at 8.30 AM. I take a glance at the WhatsApp messages also around this time.

Most of my television viewing is limited to about an

hour or so in the evening, mostly on the news. I have not seen any serials or movies on television for a very long time. Once in a while, we go to movie houses to watch movies.

Gardening

Gardening is one of my passions. I do spend Saturday mornings doing garden work, so that I keep fit and take care of the plants in our garden in the way I like to do, rather than getting it done by our gardener. Other days, I sprinkle water in the early morning on all the potted plants on the second and third floor terraces. When I take a break in the morning from writing and other work, I often go down to my garden on the ground floor to do small jobs and feel relaxed.

There is satisfaction when I see the guava trees bearing fruit. I had planted them ten years back by getting special seeds from Amazon. Even the one in the large plastic pot on my second-floor terrace has finally got a small fruit on its branch. The potted rose, Gandharaj, and Rajanigandha plants on the terrace emanate their fragrance in the winter days and evenings, and make you happy.

Songs and Music

Listening to music was another passion cultivated since high school days. More recently, I had not been listening much to my collection of music. The fifty long-playing (LP) records from my student days that I had brought to India are damaged. Of course, I had never played them on the Garard record player that I had brought back from those days. The Dynaco amplifier that I had assembled more than sixty years back was still working when I used it along with the Roland Synthesizer that I have, since the year 1992. The collection of CDs of American and Indian music is there, and I use them sparingly, a few times a month, if at all. But my BPL audio system, which I have from the year 1997, just gave up last month during the power disturbance during the Ratha yatra festival in July of this year. I have to get it fixed or buy a new system to keep listening to the CDs. I would also like to subscribe to Spotify to listen to the latest music, and especially the Sanskrit hymns.

I am regularly participating in the Odia Sanskruti, Sanskrit, and Sangeet classes that are held every Sunday from 9 AM to 11 AM for the children. Hopefully, some of that would rub me, and I could sing Bhajans and hymns!

Readings

Reading novels, stories, poems, and discussions is another passion that flares up as the situation and needs arise during retirement. No doubt, time spent on the internet and social networks has reduced the extent of reading time available. Though I am on Facebook and X, I do not spend any time there. I have a few books on my desk that I have to read. They are in English, Odia, and Hindi. They range from Sartre's novel to discourses on Buddhist Jhanas, Odia poems, and Hindi Kavyas. I hope to read them as time flows! It is always more enjoyable to read books in paper format rather than in online form!

My Zen Rituals

Zen is famous for categorizing processes into a set of clear steps to adopt and live by. I have now got my daily life into a set of steps that I take every day without thinking. This way, life becomes easy flowing, no time to ponder and think, but to live every moment only!

I get up in the morning to my alarm at 6.15 AM or before that. I walk to the bathroom, relieve myself, and then wash my face. I then go down the stairs for two floors to open the side entrance to my house and then unlock the main gate at the front of the house. I put off all the lights and then sit in the first-floor window room, sip a glass of warm water heated by the microwave oven, and listen to the radio station Cuttack to know about the news of the world around. I have to first hear the melodious renderings of the Bhagavat written by Jagannath Das, the sixteenth-century Odia poet of the Bhakti movement. I have to go through hearing the daily instructions for the farmers and the weather forecast. Then comes India and world news from Delhi, rendered in Sanskrit. In between, I sip the juices of Aloe Vera, Indian gooseberries, bitter gourd, and rose apple. I prepare a warm glass of lemon water and then drop a spoonful of turmeric and sip through that. Anuradha joins in this daily ritual at the large full windows looking out at our garden, the road in front, Akshaya Mohanty Walking Park, and the giant Ekamrakanan Park beyond that. We do sometimes catch flower thieves who come to pluck out the hibiscus flowers from our garden. We are amazed that they don't feel guilty doing this for the sake of getting blessings from the gods!

It is time now to clean up and take a bath, and then go upstairs to my terrace garden on the third floor and pluck some leaves from the holy basil tree and start chewing them. I have to water the potted plants on the third-floor terrace: flower plants of roses, Amonda, Rajanigandha, and a couple of fruit plants of guava, lemon, etc. As I water the plants, I try to receive as much of the morning sun rays on my bare chest so that I can generate enough vitamin D. Coming down the stairs to the second-floor terrace, I have to water the mix of flower and fruit plants: roses, Tagara, violet lilac, Sugandharaj, Pomegranates, sapota, etc.

Once the plants are taken care of, it is my turn to take care of my body and mind by performing some yoga asanas, pranayama, and a few minutes of meditation. These thirty minutes of daily routine are critical to keeping my body fit and flexible.

It is time now for breakfast at 8.30 AM. I have walnuts and almonds that were soaked from the previous night. I peel off the outer cover of these nuts and eat them first at my desk on the second floor. I have to go down the stairs by two floors and sit at the dining room table for breakfast. The morning newspapers, Times of India, and Dharitri (Odia) are on the table. I go through these two newspapers, as I eat my breakfast of mostly fruits of four to five varieties, depending on the season: Pomegranates, apples, guavas, papayas, watermelons, berries, Lichis, sapotas, oranges, pears, custard apples, etc. Sometimes I take half a bowl of boiled oats or Ragi and mix them with the fruits to make it more palatable.

Once breakfast is finished, I go upstairs to the window room to make a cup of black coffee or tea with the help of the microwave oven and put a few slices of ginger and a spoonful of molasses in it to make it sweet and pungent. I climb the stairs to go to my second-floor office to sit down at my desk and sip coffee or tea as I start to do some writing. The goal is to do a couple of hours of writing before noon. Once that is accomplished, it is time to look at the mail on the internet and take care of the other responsibilities of life, like meeting friends and colleagues for discussions at home or other places. This is also the free time to do any reading of the books before lunch at 2 PM.

Lunch is served at 2 PM at the dining table on the ground floor. We have vegetarian meals on Mondays and Thursdays. The other days, we mostly eat fish and chicken, rarely any red meat like mutton or lamb. Lunch consists of a little brown rice, some pulses, a vegetarian or non-veg curry, some spinach or equivalent, and a fried vegetarian mix. Anuradha is the designer of the dishes on the menu, and Soni implements them with occasional help from her.

It is afternoon nap time from about 3.30 PM to 4.30 PM, and I go upstairs to my second-floor office to sleep quietly undisturbed. The alarm rings at 5.00 PM to remind me that it is time to go down and take a stroll at the Akshaya Mohanty Park in front of my house. I walk down to the park and take about four rounds around the walking track. I will encounter only a few people walking there at that time, especially after the COVID-19 outbreak in 2020. The total run is more than 2km, and sometimes I walk in the 'Kin-Hin' (walking meditation in Zen) mode, focusing fully on the environment.

Back home after the walk in the park, it is time for tea from the dried-up hibiscus flowers that I gather after Anuradha discards them from the previous day's offerings to her gods. This herbal tea is supposed to lower cholesterol and do other good things for your health! It is also a good time to munch few nuts at this time, along with the tea.

It is 6.30 PM now, and time for the targeted meditation. I prefer this time since I am physically wide awake at this time and only need to wake up my inner self. The twenty-five minutes of meditation in the adjacent glass room next to my office on the second floor is the most restful and relaxing exercise. The evening darkness and the surrounding plants below the open blue sky contribute to a serene atmosphere, making it easier to concentrate.

I relax, take a couple of deep breaths, and then exhale to clear up any extra gas in the system. The timer on my cellphone is set for twenty-five minutes of meditation. I stretch the dark towel in front of me to provide a dark environment on the floor so that I am not distracted by my gaze during meditation. I sit on the Zafu (round pillow used in Zen meditation) in the cross-legged half lotus position, and then start counting on the timer. I almost close my eyes and bring the focus to breathing at the 'Hara', the point about two inches down from the navel. I feel the air as it fills up the lower belly, and then as the air is emptied from the lower belly during the exhaling process, I count in my mind 'one' as I breathe out. In the next cycle, as I breathe out, I count 'two' in my mind and so on, up to a count of 'ten'. Then the process of counting is repeated. I go through at least ten cycles of those counting processes.

But the focus is not on the counting, but on the breathing in and out process. Counting is just incidental to keeping the mind focused on following the breathing process. Once I go through at least five of these cycles of breathing in and out, the mind is already calm and quiet, all the extraneous thoughts have disappeared, and five to six minutes have already elapsed. There is no need to do further counting, just follow the breathing in and out, and may chant 'Om' and 'Mu' silently in the mind. The mind comes to a peaceful and silent state, and goes on to a deeper and deeper state of concentration.

I try to turn daily activities into regular rituals so that one automatically follows these steps without effort. The days move very fast this way. I follow these rituals every day except Saturday, which is a completely open day. I try to work in my gardens for a couple of hours in the morning, and do other clean-up activities within the house. That is also the day to do any shopping outside in the morning or evening. The evening is spent completely in relaxation mode, sometimes attending entertainment programs outside the house.

Further To Walk

There are always medium-term and long-term projects in the background that drive life. At this age, all of these projects are altruistic in nature and provide the juice to go on and enjoy every bit of life.

I am certainly gratified that the Government of India, along with the state governments, has taken bold steps in the world of semiconductors, computers, networks, and artificial intelligence to foster rapid developments in these areas by supporting investments from technological companies with deep skills in particular areas. I am certainly looking forward to seeing the progress in these areas in India and Odisha.

As pointed out earlier, one medium-term project has started, where the plan is to deliver a series of classes to educate youngsters on languages, culture, and the fine arts. I call this 'Jnanodaya Abhijan', because the goal is to awaken the young minds between ten to fifteen years to our culture, language, and the arts. The first batch of participants, including some elders, started on 17th August in our sangha quarters in the IRC Village house. This project has to be developed as a two-year program with two levels of classes that could be delivered to multiple batches of participants. A participant must have taken this course over a period of two to three years to achieve a desirable level of proficiency. Proficiency Certificates will be awarded on completion of the one and two-year programs. Our goal is to help establish more such centers so that these activities will have wider effects in society.

There are many medium-term writing projects

envisioned. One is to translate this book into Odia and get it published so that more people in Odisha can read it. There are more translation projects later. I have to translate into Odia, my book, 'The Buddha Reveals'.

The monthly Zen meditation sessions will continue as long as I am there. It has been ten years since this activity started at the IRC Village house, and we plan to celebrate the ten years of the sangha in December 2025. A magazine will be published on this occasion to commemorate the ten years of the Zen sangha.

Of course, we still have the desire to make a few more trips within and outside India to Lumbini and Kathmandu in Nepal, Kyoto and Nara in Japan, and Ayodhya and Varanasi in India.

One long-term project is to develop the plot that we have near Info Valley into a center of Advaita Dhyana Kalaasangha, where children and adults can participate in artistic and dharmic activities, as said earlier.

A long-term goal for myself is to further intensify and regularize my Zen rituals so that I can more deeply enjoy every aspect of life, and I stay hale and hearty for the coming years! The daily meditation sittings are definitely becoming more regular, deeper, and longer. I may or may not achieve Nirvana, but I would be on that road for as long as I breathe!

Photographs

IRC Village House with Kalinga Zen Advaita Sangha from the garden side on the ground floor, 2024

VIP Colony House, lighted during the 2023 New Year, the second-floor glass meditation room can be seen on the left side

Varish and Anuradha at Pahalgam, Kashmir, having breakfast next to the stream in the hotel, June 2024

Varish and Anuradha at Sambaleswaree Temple, Sambalpur, Dec 2024

New Year celebration at Puri beach hotel, Jan 2023

Arjun and Amrita with grandparents, Feb 2023

Amrita in the Odissi dancing pose at VIP Colony, Feb 2023

VIP Colony Front Lawn, 2023

Advaita Zen Meditation Hall, 2023

Kamakura Buddha, Zen trip by Varish, 2018

Myosin-ji Zen Garden, Zen trip by Varish, 2018

Tenryu-ji Rock Garden,
Zen trip by Varish, 2018

Kyoto River scene,
Zen trip by Varish,
2018

15 Arrowhead Drive, Branchburg, NJ; Front view

Tenryu-ji Zen Garden, Zen trip by Varish, 2018

Varish, Asit Mohanty, Amar Satpathy, Dr. Bimalendu Mohanty at Book Opening in Buddha Mandir, Bhubaneswar, 2013

Audience at Book Opening in Buddha Mandir, Doreen Schnurr and Anuradha Panigrahi in the front row from left

Back of Branchburg House, 1981

Westborough House, winter 1985

NIT Rourkela trip to Daringibadi, Sept 2023

NIT Rourkela trip with batchmates, February 2023

Dinner meeting with school and college classmates in Balangir, 1983

Anuradha and Varish in Las Vegas, 1973

N3-B6, IRC Village House, 1998

IIT Kharagpur Electronics 1968 batchmates

Arun and Swapna with my mother-in-law Hemlata Padhi, 2009

Arun and Swapna with my sister-in-law Sushama Pathy,
Dr. Shastri Panchagnula, and Jyothika Panchagnula
at VIP Colony house, 2009

Gautam Padhi (1950 – 1970) of Kolkata (Anuradha's brother)

Bhagavan Panigrahi (1949 – 1972) of Balangir (my eldest nephew and son of my eldest brother, Koramoni Panigrahi)

Arun with my father-in-law,
Bhagirathi Padhi (1911 – 2004) of Kolkata, 1988

Arun and Swapna with Padma C Panigrahi (1932 – 2015)
of Berhampur (my 2nd brother) and Pratap Pathy of Kolkata
(my brother-in-law)

Rupa C. Panigrahi (1936 – 2025) of Bodoboranga (my 3rd brother)

Subasini Panda (1928 – 2010) of Chiladi (my sister)

THE INDIAN WHO MOVED BACK | 279

Koramoni Panigrahi
(1922 – 1987) of Balangir
(my eldest brother)

Hema Panigrahi (1904 – 1985)
of Bodoboranga (my mother)

Bodoboranga village, the row house on the far right of about 10 feet wide, is our ancestral house built by my father

Black Eagle Books

www.blackeaglebooks.org
info@blackeaglebooks.org

Black Eagle Books, an independent publisher, was founded as a nonprofit organization in April, 2019. It is our mission to connect and engage the Indian diaspora and the world at large with the best of works of world literature published on a collaborative platform, with special emphasis on foregrounding Contemporary Classics and New Writing.

www.ingramcontent.com/pod-product-compliance
Lightning Source LLC
Chambersburg PA
CBHW060553080526
44585CB00013B/553